Ladle

YOU'RE IN CONTROL

YOU'RE IN CONTROL

A Guide for
Latter-day Saint
Youth

RON WOODS

Deseret Book
Salt Lake City, Utah

First printing August 1986

Library of Congress Cataloging-in-Publication Data

Woods, Ron.
    You're in control.

    Includes index.
    Summary: Demonstrates for young people, particularly
those of The Church of Jesus Christ of Latter-day
Saints, how to manage their time, set goals, and enjoy
a successful, enriched life.
    1. Spiritual life—Mormon authors.   2. Youth—
Religious life.   3. Youth—Conduct of life.   [1. Time
management.   2. Conduct of life.   3. Church of Jesus
Christ of Latter-day Saints.   4. Mormon Church]
I. Title.
BX8656.W66   1986   245.4'8933203   86-16532
ISBN 0-87579-046-1

To Zina

CONTENTS

PREFACE

Sitting down to read a book that tells you how to take control of your life is a little like watching those very long TV commercials that come on late at night. They promise that you—even you—*especially* you—can become an instant millionaire if you will attend an upcoming investment seminar—payment in advance. The idea is appealing, but skepticism runs high.

So, why should you read a book that raises that same skepticism by promising you equally fantastic results? Well, unlike the late-night commercials, this book doesn't promise instant perfection. Most of the concepts described here will require practice and commitment to make them work. Good things aren't instant. But look at the following list of skills this book will help you acquire, then see if these skills aren't worth a little effort. You will learn how to

- assume responsibility for your life and enjoy the exhilaration of facing life's challenges.
- find true success in life, the kind that brings you real happiness, not just praise or some other fleeting external.
- make plans and projections that will lead you to where you want to go in the future.
- manage time so that you don't feel pressured but get those things done that you find worthwhile.
- schedule your work so you are aiming at *your* deadlines, not someone else's.
- set goals that put *you* in charge of your own life rather than always working for someone else.
- use the examples and advice of parents, teachers, and friends to the utmost.
- plan your life so there's time for guilt-free leisure as well as work and accomplishment.

I'm convinced that most young people are interested in making the best use of their time, in being successful, and especially in taking control of their own lives rather than leaving that control to outside forces. There are simple principles for each of these goals. They're not magic, and they require effort, but these principles really do work. They will give your life direction, help you use your time to the best advantage, and make your work easier—or, viewed another way, they will help you do better work in the same amount of time. Best of all, they will make you the boss of yourself.

If you don't feel the necessity for any of these ideas, you may not think you need this book at the moment. I wouldn't throw it away though. There will come a day when you start to wonder where your life is headed, how in the world to accomplish all those things you want to do, and whether all the demands on your time are worth the trouble. This out-of-control feeling comes to most people at times, making us temporarily full of self-doubts and questions about the value of our efforts.

That's when you need to recall where you tossed this book. It could come in handy right about then by showing you how to put some direction in your life and by persuading you that you—even you—*especially* you—can be a colossal success in the most important things in life.

1
ACHIEVEMENT:
What Success Is
and What It Isn't

To a small child, success is finding where mom hid the cookie jar. To the president of the United States, signing an international agreement after difficult negotiations may constitute success. But no matter how people may differ in their definition and measurement of it, we all agree that success is a good thing to have. Wanting to succeed—wanting things to turn out in a desirable way—is a common hope of humanity.

Certainly not everyone wants to be a superstar with the acclaim of the world, because not everyone wants that kind of attention. But we all want to succeed at those things that are important to us, even if others aren't aware of our accomplishments. Fame may not be the goal, but the satisfaction of valid achievement is.

In determining what success really is, it's helpful to note that some successes come as gifts and some as wages. Naturally, the gifts come easily. At an early age, Sue discovered that she could, without really trying, make people relax, feel good, and laugh. People just seemed to feel better in her presence. Sue's smile and natural self-confidence put others at ease and made it simple for her to make friends. Without any real effort on her part, she enjoyed success in human relations.

Perhaps, like Sue, most people have a valuable trait that comes naturally to them. With no apparent effort—sometimes without thinking about it at all—they can perform or accomplish something that others have to work hard to attain. This kind of success is like a gift they've been given. Probably you'll be able to think of areas of competence in your own life that come easily to you.

If all our successes were gifts, there would be no need for goals, hard work, determination, or any of the other principles in this book. And though it's human nature to want things to be easy, we usually feel prouder of those accomplishments we had to sweat over. Our sometimes lazy natures might prefer otherwise, but most of the time, our attainments will not come as gifts. It's a fact of life that the majority of our successes will be wages—wages received for hard effort expended.

Take the case of Tom who found that he was not a naturally gifted athlete. While several of his friends seemed to have innate abilities in sports, Tom had to work hard to make second-string. But he did work hard, and though he felt disappointed that he didn't make first-string, he was still proud that he had come as far as he had.

Like Tom, we all have areas that aren't easy for us, areas where we have to work for everything we get. Sometimes we decide that attaining a goal in one of these difficult fields isn't worth the trouble; it's too much effort compared to the reward of achievement, which may be far in the future. At other times we say, "No matter what it takes, I'm going to make that goal." Then we work at the task until we succeed—and how great we feel when we do. One of the sweetest feelings in life is the savoring of a success that cost us dearly in terms of time, effort, and sweat. In those moments, we know our commitment paid off, and the warm glow of victory is the only reward we need.

This book is about success—what it is, whether it's worth it, how to get it, and how to keep it. Specifically, this book is about *your* success—the personalized achievements that define success for you, regardless of what others may do.

Your Life Is Your Responsibility

One of the first steps toward achieving success in life is recognizing that each person is in charge of himself. But some people have a lot of trouble with this. For example, Julie seemed unable to accept that any of the good things in her life could be due to her own efforts. When she got a good grade on a school paper, she assumed she was just lucky in her choice of a subject that the teacher sympathized with. She wasn't able to accept that her success was due to her own efforts. When Julie received a *bad* grade on a test, on the other hand, she felt that she should have studied harder. She had no trouble accepting her failures as her own fault.

Joe viewed life in a different way. He heartily congratulated himself on his successes and blamed anybody and everybody else when he failed. To him, a good grade on an essay meant that he had done a superior job of writing, while a poor test score meant that the teacher had created a stupid exam. While Joe felt his successes were due to his own brilliance, he seemed unable to accept that perhaps he might not have failed if he'd worked to attain a better result. Notice that Joe was the opposite of Julie in accepting responsibility for success and rejecting blame for failure.

Actually, Julie and Joe's responses aren't too surprising in light of research studies that indicate there is a tendency for males in our culture to blame bad luck or other outside forces when things go wrong and to take the credit when things go right. Females, on the other hand, tend to blame themselves when things go wrong and credit good luck or other outside forces when things turn out right. Of course, these very interesting tendencies aren't true of everyone.

Additional studies show there are two basic types of people: those who think they are the master of their own destiny, and those who think outside forces control them. Consider for a moment which type you are.

Do you generally work toward goals you want, or do you sit back and wait to get lucky, hoping for your wishes to be granted by some outside force? Do you find yourself blaming teachers, parents, friends, enemies, inflation, the Russians, or the neighbor's black cat when your plans go awry? Do you accept your strengths as well as your weaknesses? Are you willing to take the blame for things that go wrong in your plans as well as the credit when something turns out right? Or do you regard it as luck in either case? Certainly there are elements of life we cannot control. Life does bring surprises. But how aware are you of all those things you *can* control?

Bill was a young man who had always been able to find a convenient excuse for failure. School problems were blamed on his parents for asking him to do chores that took time away from his schoolwork, on his little brothers and sisters for making noise while he tried to study, or on his teachers for not making assignments clear. In family disputes, he avoided the real issues by blaming his parents for not understanding him. Bill never seemed able to accept how he contributed to his own problems.

Bill had only his final project left to complete in order to attain his Eagle Scout rank, but for two years, he never seemed to get the proposal written up and sent in for approval. Bill's parents reminded and encouraged him but didn't push him, because they wanted this achievement to be his, not theirs. They felt that part of the value of completing the Eagle rank, or any other difficult accomplishment, is in showing the maturity to carry through on a project to completion.

Whenever his parents would ask Bill about his project and encourage him to set a deadline to send in the application, he would list his many impressive excuses for not getting the task done. In a sense, they were all valid reasons. School had kept him quite busy. The Varsity Scout coach hadn't picked up the forms from the Scout office for a few weeks. The city official hadn't mailed him the list he'd requested of the parks that needed improving. Each day after school, Bill hadn't remembered to phone again for the map before the office closed. There were plenty of reasons to blame others.

But one day Bill came to the realization that while these points were all valid, they hadn't actually prevented him from doing his Eagle project. He was just hiding behind them. It became clear that he wasn't too busy to do these tasks one step at a time. Bill knew he could have gotten the forms and the list himself if he had simply decided to do so. He saw that he could overcome each of these delays and problems if he really wanted the Eagle rank, and that the decision was up to him. In coming to this realization, Bill had taken a big step toward accepting responsibility for his own success in life. There comes a time when we must stop blaming others for our failures and shortcomings, forget the past, and stand up and take charge of our own future.

When he took the initiative, Bill was surprised that his parents, his Scout leaders, and the city officials all seemed more cooperative than before. Whether this was really the case, or just his new perception of the situation, it seemed to Bill that the willingness of others to help increased *after* he accepted responsibility and took charge of his own project.

It's sometimes surprising how interested teachers, leaders, and parents are in supporting the view that you are responsible for your own life. You may find that statement hard to believe, since some of these people may have seemed like Marine drill sergeants intent on directing your every step.

But their behavior is usually based on the fact that they have not seen you taking responsibility for yourself. Or it may be that they don't always notice when you *do* accept responsibility; sometimes adults are a little slow to see these things. But as you show your increasing ability to make wise decisions and take control, you'll see that people are willing to give more and more of that control to you. You'll become partners with these adults interested in your life, and they'll be anxious to concede that it's really you that is in charge.

Unlikely? Try it. If parents seem slow to turn responsibility over to you, remember that while it's natural for you to demand more freedom, it's just as natural for parents to try to hold on to their family and to see you as their "baby." These differing perspectives create some degree of tension in the family, and as you grow older and show responsibility for your decisions, this tension needs periodic adjustment.

The way to make that adjustment—and handle other tensions, incidentally—is not to rebel and make demands but simply to talk with your parents about your feelings. In a kind way, try telling them that you recognize that it's *your* job to handle the task at hand, and that you are ready to do so. Tell them that you will welcome their advice and help. Such a statement will greatly impress parents and assure them that you are ready to take responsibility for your life.

You know by now that I think you'd be better off believing that you have a major control over your destiny, and that you ought to take hold of the steering wheel and drive your life in the direction you want it to go. That's what *I* think—but what do *you* think? It's your choice, and no one can make the decision for you. If you've already felt the power such a view gives you, you know why I want it for you. It's a great way to live. But if you haven't yet tried taking control to this extent, you're in for one great feeling as you come to realize the strength that comes to one who is in charge.

This approach doesn't imply a rejection of appropriate help, advice, and direction from others, including your parents. But the idea that you are responsible for your own basic direction in life is a critical view of the world. Sadly, this is a concept that some never experience; they're always waiting for their ship to come in instead of pushing a canoe into the surf and paddling out to meet it.

At some point, if you are to be successful in life, you will have to decide that it's really all up to you. Not that others can't help you, but you can't expect anyone else to carve your path through the steamy jungle. Acceptance of that fact is a vital step on the road to success. Life is all up to you.

Don't Let Life Happen; Make It Happen

Every pancake has two sides, and this "take charge" attitude has an alternative, but not a very appealing one. It's the "why worry?" approach to life. This philosophy means waiting around to see where the wind blows. Like a stowaway down in the hold, those who have the "why worry?" attitude will let someone else be the captain up on the quarterdeck. Since we can't control everything, and there are bound to be surprises in life no matter how much we plan, such a view might have some initial appeal. "Why worry?" this view says. "Nothing's going to work out right anyway."

Some Latter-day Saint youths have taken this idea to a disturbing extreme. Based on hearsay that the Millennium must be coming soon—or nuclear war, or *something*—they say, "Why make any plans?" It's as if any efforts at self-improvement would somehow be wasted. Well, that idea is at least as old as the New Testament, where those who were shortsighted stated it in this form: "Eat, drink, and be merry. . . ." This implies that there was no need to do more than live for the moment because tomorrow would wipe out all their hopes and plans anyway. This view was wrong then, and it's wrong now.

Yet the idea still attracts some because it appears easy. However, such an approach is only easy at the moment. In the long run, it's a lot harder because inevitably there are regrets. People look back and say, "What if I had gone to college or prepared myself better for marriage or . . . ?" And often, by then, it's too late to go back and change the situation.

No, it's easier to live with mistakes, knowing we did our best at the time, than to live with regrets about missing opportunities. In the latter case, we always have to wonder what would have happened if we had not neglected, delayed, and avoided some of the tough decisions in our earlier years. The strange thing is that we can't stop making decisions. Life has a way of continuing to happen whether we want it to or not, and if we don't make certain decisions, they will make themselves.

Paul didn't decide to start his term paper until two nights before the due date. Although he got the paper finished, his work was poor because he didn't make the decision to begin early enough. By delaying, he lost his chance to make a different decision about the outcome. By not deciding, he had let the decision make itself and simply had to accept the poor results. There's an old saying that when you pick up one end of a stick, you pick up the other end too. Paul's delay brought him the same result as if he had *chosen* to do a poor term paper.

A good student isn't working only for the teacher when he does a term paper. He should be working for himself. He *is* working for himself when he decides to make the paper a meaningful project by accepting responsibility for his own learning and consequently for his own growth.

We can't escape decisions. We make them even when we try to avoid them, and every decision we don't make, or make by default, has a result. For instance, if you think you want to be a doctor but don't decide to do everything necessary to become one, it won't happen. Few medical school deans will come knocking on your door. You will have to knock on their door, and they will expect you to have done some preparation first. By not determining well in advance to make that preparation, the result is the same as if you had decided not to become a doctor.

If you think *maybe* you want a temple marriage, but don't commit to settle for nothing less, that probably won't happen, unless you're lucky enough to meet a person who is determined to take you there. In such matters, however, luck isn't enough. Trusting your life to luck means you're not really in charge, and the odds are against you. It's the same as deciding not to marry in the temple. Is it worth the risk?

Saying you'll *probably* go on a mission without deciding to prepare for it spiritually, morally, and financially will cause the preparation time to be lost, and that time won't be fully recoverable. You may be able to get your life in order and accept the call, but you'll be out there regretting your lost preparation time as you knock on doors. Some returned missionaries will tell you that they managed to overcome that lost time, but you're not likely to find one who recommends delaying the early decision to go on a mission and the subsequent planning for a successful mission.

So it is with many things in life. When we choose the start of a path, we also choose the end of it. There comes a day when the preparation time is past and we must stand on what we've done. Those who have taken charge of themselves stand a lot taller on such days. The choice today is whether to decide to decide.

Doing What *You* Care About; Finding Your Own Way

Surveys show that people who are asked to define success almost always mention money or fame. While these two items might be nice to have at times, they don't necessarily constitute success in life. Actually, they have nothing to do with true success unless an individual wants them and chooses them as part of his definition of success.

One of the most common delusions is that we're successful only if others call us successful. Success, we suppose, is a label that's applied to us by other people. Such thinking confuses success with fame and acclaim. Since we all need some degree of recognition and appreciation from others, it's easy to find ourselves seeking the spotlight and straining to hear the applause. In some cases, we start to need that outside praise to feel good about ourselves. Our self-esteem has then become dependent on the views of others.

Fame isn't a bad thing, though its results are bad for many when they find they must have applause to accomplish anything. They're actually working for the wrong reason, and when the acclaim fades—as acclaim always does—they're left with ashes. Numerous are the stories of famous, rich, respected people who are miserably unhappy. The world calls them successful, but they're failures in their personal lives. They haven't learned to live for the right reasons. No, fame isn't to be confused with success. For, while it's possible for a person to have his or her most meaningful accomplishments recognized and applauded by the world, such a thing isn't likely nor is it necessary. The frustrating thing about working toward fame and recognition is that such things are mostly out of your control. You can't force people to applaud you, so you're constantly worrying about the wrong thing, about whether your achievements are going to be noticed and accepted. Worrying about something you have no control over is self-defeating and fatiguing.

A great college football player can't fret about whether he will win the Heisman Trophy. If he does, he's worrying about something that's out of his hands, and this worrying will distract him from the things he *can* do something about, such as perfecting his game skills. Even if you could do something about public acceptance, your goals would soon lose their meaning to you if you always worried about public approval. You've then altered your goals from doing those things that bring a feeling of achievement, to those that bring applause. The applause itself then becomes your goal.

On the other hand, the beauty of working toward real success—the kind that matters, whether recognized by the world or not—is that you can control and measure your own progress through goal setting and self-evaluation. Worrying about acceptance isn't necessary because hard work and proper goals will take you where you want to go. Then your definition of success doesn't depend on recognition from others.

If success isn't worldly acclaim, what is it? I define success as *accomplishing those things that matter most to you.* Think about that idea. If you spend your life doing things other than those that matter to you personally, how can that be success, no matter how much money or fame you attain? Conversely, if you feel good about your accomplishments, how can that be failure even though the world may not recognize your achievements?

As you mature, you must realize the need to do those things that are right for *you,* whether the world agrees or not. You must, in the end, feel good about yourself and what you've done with your life. If you have worthy goals and are progressing toward their accomplishment, you will feel good about yourself. Self-confidence grows from accomplishment, and as your self-confidence grows, you find you can accomplish even more. This is a never-ending cycle, a growth cycle, and it feels good.

Success Equals Greater Freedom

"I don't see why I have to do this stupid algebra. I don't like it, I don't understand it, and I will never use it in any way in real life." Most parents and schoolteachers have had to respond to a statement like this from one or more of their offspring or students. There are numerous ways to respond to such a statement, whether the statement is about algebra, history, chemistry, doing the dishes, weeding the garden, or helping paint the kitchen. The poorest response is something along the lines of "Do what you're told, kid, or I'll double the assignment." Next worst is, "Do well in math, and you can grow up and earn a lot of money." Better is, "If you work hard at this task, you'll eventually feel good about mastering algebra." But perhaps the best response is, "The more you know and the more you can do, the greater will be your freedom."

Have you ever thought about the freedom you gain by being able to do more? Some miss the point and think that a hardworking student is enslaved and chained to the desk all the time. The fact is that such a student is actually increasing his freedom, now or in the future, through the choices his knowledge gives him. If he gets good grades and another student doesn't, who will have the greater choice of what to do after graduation?

A very narrow definition of freedom is the opportunity to do everything we want. Actually that's chaos and anarchy. A more meaningful definition of freedom is the opportunity to become what we want to become. One helpful viewpoint is that there are lesser freedoms and greater freedoms. Many people are willing to settle for the lesser. The freedom to watch TV all evening before the big test is a lesser freedom. Choosing to turn the TV off to prepare for the test so as to gain knowledge, good grades, and the choice of which college to attend or which profession to enter, prepares one for a greater freedom. Of course, like all decisions, this one has a cost: missing the TV show. But a lesser cost has been paid for a greater freedom, and in the long run, it's a pretty small cost.

Look at the following choices that virtually all of us face or will face; notice the lesser freedoms lost and the greater freedoms gained:

Choice Made: to stay morally clean
Lesser Freedom Lost: the thrill of the moment
Greater Freedom Gained: worthiness for eternal marriage

Choice Made: healthy eating and exercise
Lesser Freedom Lost: indulgence
Greater Freedom Gained: health, vigor, vitality, strength, endurance

Choice Made: to keep up on homework
Lesser Freedom Lost: TV time, activities with friends
Greater Freedom Gained: better grades, more knowledge and understanding of the world, more insights into and preparation for various fields of work, more options for advanced training

Choice Made: to never cheat
Lesser Freedom Lost: getting an easy grade on a quiz
Greater Freedom Gained: self-esteem and pride in getting an honest grade

Choice Made: to help other people in need
Lesser Freedom Lost: time for personal activities
Greater Freedom Gained: warm feeling of love and concern for others, insight into one of the main purposes of life, growth as a selfless person

The list could go on indefinitely since we all face numerous choices each day. Sometimes both choices might be lesser (deciding which of two types of pizza to order) or both might be greater (deciding whether to spend time reading to a blind man or planting flowers in a widow's yard). But more often than not, it's a matter of lesser versus greater, and the distinction is usually clear when we look at the situation.

Another way to state this idea is that we sometimes have to give up something at the moment to gain a greater value in the future. Ten years from now, there won't be any great deprivation recalled for giving up a particular TV show, but you might feel cheated if so much time was spent with the tube, to the exclusion of studies, that you end up in a lifework that is less than you preferred. Therefore, choices can often be based on this question: Will my selection increase or decrease my freedom? Thinking of our choices, large and small, in this way helps us as we consider the many daily opportunities before us.

Therefore, try not to bristle at parents and teachers who may sound too directive at times but are just trying to help you see that you can squander your choices on the relatively lesser gratifications of the moment, or you can invest in the greater values of the future. They're trying to be sure you understand that if something doesn't give you greater freedom, either now or in the future, it's not likely the thing for you. If you've figured that out for yourself by now, then tell your parents about it, and they probably won't feel compelled to keep reminding you of this principle all the time.

Conclusion

Success is what we're after, not in the way the world defines it, as fame or money, but as achievement in those things that matter most to us. Only we can decide what we want to accomplish in life. As we accept that responsibility, we start to see that the daily choices we make lead us closer to or further from what we really want. When we apply the idea that our choices increase or decrease our real, meaningful freedoms, then we have a guide for decision making that can lead us in the right direction.

Life keeps coming at us. We have a choice: either sit down and watch it go by, or jump up and join the parade. Each of us can make the choice to succeed; the first step is nothing more and nothing less than the desire to do so.

2
SELF-WORTH:
Your Inestimable Value

Before I tell you about a young man named Grant, let's get some definitions clear—the definitions of self-worth, self-image, and self-esteem. These are three terms that are often used interchangeably, but they do differ in meaning. The definitions of these terms will help you understand our discussion about your self-worth.

Self-worth is the intrinsic value of a person. It isn't dependent on how much he can do or how well he can do it. Self-worth is just a way of saying a person is a child of God, and therefore valuable. No one can change or reduce a person's self-worth. Regardless of how anyone else views an individual, his self-worth is a fact.

Self-image (or self-concept), on the other hand, is the view a person has of himself, be it negative or positive. Some people have a low self-image because they fail to properly recognize their own self-worth. Self-image, then, is simply the way people view their self-worth.

Self-esteem (or self-respect) is a *positive* self-image. This means to value and esteem self to the point of having confidence in one's abilities and a satisfaction with one's actions. It's the ultimate goal, the way of correctly viewing self-worth, the desirable self-image for the success-bound person.

Now that the definitions for these terms are clear, let's look at a high-school student named Grant.

"How does Brother Welch know me so well?" Grant marveled, as he read again the note he'd received a few moments earlier from his seminary teacher. He could tell from the excessive stillness in the classroom and the serious expressions on the faces of the other students that many of them were wondering the same thing as they read their handwritten notes. How could Brother Welch possibly know so much about each individual in his class?

The lesson that day had been about how people ought to learn to know their own strengths and to use them to be successful. Then Brother Welch said, "I've taken a little time to write each of you an assessment of what I believe your individual strengths and weaknesses are. We've been together in class only a few weeks, but I think I know a little about each one of you, so I hope no one will be offended that I've made these observations." Then he passed out the notes.

Grant looked at his note again. Certain phrases jumped out at him: "Often doubt your own abilities . . . anxious to please but sometimes fearful to try . . . shy about starting new friendships . . . afraid to reveal true feelings for fear that people might reject you . . . desirous of succeeding in life but often unsure of how to do it." These and similar phrases seemed such an accurate picture of Grant, yet he had always thought he hid this side of his personality under a confident exterior. How could Brother Welch have seen through him so well?

After the students had a moment to ponder, Brother Welch asked, "How many of you feel I figured you out pretty well, especially your weaknesses?" Nearly every hand went up. "Well, I think I did too," he said. "Now here's the second part of the exercise. Please exchange notes with someone near you—anyone." Grant thought he couldn't have heard right. Exchange notes with just anyone in the class? Grant certainly didn't want someone else to read the note that revealed his own doubts and weaknesses so well.

"I know it sounds startling, but trust me," Brother Welch urged. "Trade notes with someone." The class members looked around anxiously, but no one made a move to trade.

"Come on, Janean," Brother Welch said as he stepped to a girl sitting in front of Grant and teasingly extracted her note from her hand. He passed Janean's note to Grant, at the same time handing Grant's note to Janean. Others were now more willing to pass their notes to those nearby.

"Read these notes, please," Brother Welch said. Grant started to read but looked up in surprise at the words he read.

There must be some mistake. Small gasps came from a few students who were experiencing the same feeling.

"Now, trade notes with someone else. Quickly." This time people were quicker to trade the notes they held. Grant read the note of a boy in back of him and couldn't believe his eyes. It couldn't be: all three notes were identical. Then he chuckled as he started to see the point.

"Students," Brother Welch began, "we come to the real lesson for today. I apologize for tricking you, in a sense, when I said I had written a personal note to each of you. It's true that I wrote each one by hand—so they were personal in that sense—but as is now obvious, all the notes are identical. And the amazing thing is that you all felt that they spoke directly to you."

The teacher paused a moment for the idea to sink in and then went on. "Isn't it astounding that these notes, which clearly emphasize feelings of self-doubt and inadequacy, are so universal that they apply to everyone, although when you first read them, each of you felt that I had found your very own personal, secret weaknesses. What do you make of this?" Brother Welch then led the class in a discussion of his main point: Feeling inadequate isn't unusual after all; almost all people doubt their own abilities.

"So, keep in mind," Brother Welch concluded at the sound of the bell, "whenever you feel doubtful about yourself, that this feeling is perfectly normal. All of us—absolutely *all* of us—have self-doubts, but the great thing is that we can succeed in spite of them." After one of the most stimulating lessons he'd ever heard, Grant left the seminary classroom that day with new insights into his potential and much greater confidence in his ability to achieve. (Idea from Terry Welch, instructor, LDS Seminaries and Institutes.)

Often people who haven't had such insight feel that their doubts are unique and that they are not capable of achieving success. "It might happen to others," they say, "but not to me. I don't have what it takes." The big secret, as Grant learned, is that we all have doubts in numerous areas. Some of the world's most successful people have self-image problems and often doubt their abilities. Yet they're still successful because they have enough faith to keep trying, and in doing so, they've taught themselves that they can succeed in spite of their doubts.

A few people have constant doubts about their worth in many or all areas and never feel good about anything they do. These people have severe self-esteem problems. Somewhere along the road of life they have learned to think of themselves as failures. They're sure they can't achieve, and that they are of little worth. They're wrong on all of these counts, but I suspect that my saying so won't convince them. These people might need professional counseling to improve their view of themselves.

But occasional or even frequent self-doubts are perfectly normal. It's a most unusual person who never doubts himself. Most of us, especially by the time we reach our teens, have such feelings rather frequently. I think there are definite reasons why this pattern is as normal as rain on Easter.

As children, we often had feelings of failure, because we had to learn to do so many things and we didn't do them very well at first. We were introduced to hundreds of new tasks within just a few years, and it's not surprising that we didn't immediately succeed at all of them. Social skills, obedience, chores, even walking and talking, all had to be mastered at an early age. Instructions, orders, directions, and requests literally bombarded us. Sometimes the things we were asked to learn were fun and interesting. Sometimes they were dreadfully boring. But that didn't let us out of them; we were still expected to do a good job.

But here's the catch: we weren't good at *all* of these things, especially in the early stages. Actually it's doubtful just how much that fact would have bothered us, except for one thing. People made a point of telling us from time to time about our shortcomings—and not always in a kindly way. Teachers and parents, not satisfied with our first efforts at some task—because their job was to get us to improve—urged us to "do it right," "try harder," or "keep at it." In doing so they often sounded more critical than they meant to. "Oh, come on, you can do it; try harder," may have been meant as an encouragement by the speaker, but it may have been perceived as criticism by a child who thought he was already trying his best. Instead of teaching us a task, these words may have been teaching us something else: that we were dumb, slow, or incapable.

For these reasons we may have started at early ages to feel

that we were of little value. Since praise came when we did something right, we probably made a false assumption—that worth was tied to achievement. If we didn't do things well, we weren't worthy people. It's a false idea, but how were we to know?

So the bad news is that childhood can be very rough on self-esteem. But where there's bad news, there's often good news as well. And in this case, the good news comes in two parts. The first is that your feelings are absolutely normal. That, I think, is some comfort. If others feel the same way and still succeed, you can too.

The second fact is just as helpful: your views of yourself can change. Self-esteem can grow. It may not be easy, but your views can be altered, a little at a time, as you see how capable and worthy you are. Let's start right now.

God Loves You

Isn't it odd that we seem so obnoxious to one another at times, but that God can always stand us? Has it occurred to you that we must be worth a great deal if God loves each of us? Some of us have never stopped to consider that God doesn't just love humankind in the abstract; he actually loves each and every one of us—warts, hangnails, and all. The fact that he created the earth and sent us to live on it must mean that he cares for us. "But," you might say, "the world could be a much better place. If he really cares for me, why is life so hard some-times?"

It's not a bad question. In fact, it's the question of the ages. Most people have asked that question many times, and philoso-phers have sought answers to it for centuries. So obviously there is no quick, easy answer. But think about it this way: If part of our purpose on earth is to be tested and to grow, then how much interference to protect us from this or that could God make in our lives and still allow the test and the growth to go on? How much intercession could he effect and yet leave us with the free agency to make our own choices and to reap the consequences of those choices?

Of course, there are times when God does intercede. But if he were to do so too often and too conspicuously, the plan would be ruined. He must let us bear the consequences of the choices we, and others, make. Otherwise, how could we learn from those consequences? As a nutshell answer to a huge philosophical question, his concern for your free agency is why he doesn't make your life easier. Always remember why you're on earth. In large part, it's to learn and grow. To me, that statement has very big implications: we must be capable of handling whatever comes our way, or why would God ask it of us?

We all make mistakes, that's true. But God doesn't judge us by how well we achieve, only by whether we try and whether our hearts are right. That's how God is different from most everybody else we know. People tend to judge others by how well they do certain things: how well they pass a football, how much math they can do, how much money they make, or some other achievement-oriented measure. But God doesn't think like that. He doesn't love us because of achievements. He just loves us because we're his children.

Since that's the case, then you must be an acceptable human being after all. You have value in God's eyes, and he wants you to see in yourself the same potential he sees there. Many individuals throughout history have made great leaps in self-esteem when they've realized this one fact: in spite of their weaknesses and even their deliberate sins, God still loves them. With that knowledge, their sights are lifted and they become partners with him in working toward the same goal: their ultimate success in life in the things that really matter.

Others Love You

Think of all the people who are interested in your life: parents, teachers, family members, church leaders, friends. Sometimes they don't say it or even show it very well, but you know they love you and that they're interested in your happiness. Furthermore, the people who know you best and love you most don't even worry about how well you perform. Their love isn't based on your accomplishments.

Over the years, I've attended plenty of baseball, soccer, football, and basketball games where my kids were participating. The relatively small crowd at these events—often just parents of the players—makes it easy to hear lots of sideline comments. Some of these comments are supportive: "That's the way to try, Jed; you'll hit it next time." "Good slide, Kevin." "Way to run, Sue." Unfortunately, there is also another brand of comment: "Aw, Jared, don't strike at junk like that." "Patrick, hold on to that ball; don't be such a fumble-fingers." "Oh, use your head, Eric; that was a stupid play." Obviously comments of this type, coming from what I call "bleacher-bleaters," seem to be much more than just helpful suggestions for improvement. To the person hearing such comments, it's more like a personal attack—and in front of his or her friends, no less.

Now, I don't know what kind of parents these people are. Obviously their performance as parents can't be judged by a few comments they may make in the heat of emotion over a sporting event. But I do worry about the effect these comments have on their youth. The message these parents seem to be giving their children is that they will be loved as long as they achieve, as long as they win. I don't think that's what is meant, but that's the message that often seems to come through.

It may be that you too have heard a lot of these negative messages in your own life. But the fact is that you are a worthy person regardless of success, achievement, or accomplishment. The irony is that as soon as you fully accept the truth that success isn't the measure of your worth and that failing at something doesn't make you a lesser person, you will gain greater power to succeed. In other words, as your self-image—the way you see yourself—improves, you will become more true to your actual self-worth—what and who you really are.

In spite of the way those "bleacher-bleaters" sound when they are yelling "encouragements," they truly do love their children and are trying to offer support. And there are many people who are able to view us as worthy people, entirely separate from our achievements, just as God does. The world in general may judge us by how well we perform, but not everybody does. Your family and your real friends will love you whether or not you're an A student, a sports hero, or a celebrity.

If you choose to believe those people who accept you for the worthy person that you are, you will grow in acceptance of your self-worth.

Accepting Yourself

Now, if God loves you and others love you, does that fact make it easier for you to love and accept yourself? It should. If not, either you doubt the soundness of the opinions of your friends—not to mention God—or you think they don't really know you very well. I believe there are three reasons why we have trouble seeing worth in ourselves.

The first reason is that we know ourselves so well. We know our own shortcomings better than anyone else does, so we are tougher on ourselves, but the fact is that all of us have faults in abundance. Even the best people have loads of them. Everyone struggles with his or her failings and problems. They're part of life. They don't ever go away, except temporarily. In the garden of life, when we get one weed hoed, another pops up. That's just the way life is. If you can accept struggles as a continuous part of growth, they'll be less frustrating. Then they're seen as challenges to be overcome and mastered, not as millstones around your neck that are dragging you down. Someone said, "If something doesn't kill you outright, it will make you better." Take that attitude about problems, and you'll look back and thank them for helping you grow.

Find your good points. Even one is enough to start with. If you can do one thing well—not perfectly, just well—you can learn to do other things well. Start where you are. Accept yourself, as God accepts you and as your family and real friends do—not in an egotistical, self-adoring way, but in a way that says, "I'm an OK person." It's a decision. If you can decide to accept yourself as you are and to go onward and upward from there, you'll succeed at the important things in life, no matter how steep the climb now appears.

The second reason why some people can't accept themselves is because of a sin they've committed or a general feeling that they are sinful people. They carry such a load of guilt that they can't accept anything good about themselves. Guilt has a purpose; specific guilt over a particular problem is a tool God uses to get us to want to do better. But there's also useless guilt. This kind doesn't cause us to improve; it just gnaws at us like a dog working on an old bone.

General guilt doesn't come from God, because it keeps us feeling worthless and thinking we can't succeed. So if you need to straighten out something in your life, do it. Settle your past and get on with your life. Refuse to be controlled and held down by guilt.

The third thing that ruins people's estimation of themselves is that they compare themselves to others. It's like the rich man who is surrounded by everything money can buy, yet still moans, "I would be happy with what I have if not for the fact that someone else might have more."

Constant comparison is destructive to happiness. There will always be someone who has more, is better looking, is more famous, or can do this or that better than you can. Try to forget the competition. Better still, don't even consider other people as competitors. Life isn't an Olympic race with winners and losers. In the race for the things that matter, we can all be winners.

Once you accept yourself as a person of worth, you can better accept others. When you realize that they aren't competitors and threats, you can accept them as they are. As you do this, you will find ways to be of greater service to your fellow beings, and this service and helpfulness will again increase your own feelings of self-worth. It's a cycle.

The cycle can be entered at any point. A person doesn't have to wait until he feels good about himself. He can start from the service end, which will cause him to start feeling better about himself, which then cycles him into doing even greater service, which makes him feel even better about his worth—and on it goes.

Though we never admit this fact at the time, we often criticize others because it makes us feel better about our own faults. If we can drag someone else down, we feel a little higher on the mountain ourselves. Of course, that's self-deception in the extreme, because we merely pull ourselves down with them. The greatest people are able to truly rejoice in the success of others.

The knowledge that everyone has faults galore, that long-term guilt is dangerous, and that comparison is harmful ought to help you know that you can succeed as a worthy person. Don't reject yourself because of poor achievement or lack of what the world calls success. All of that will pass. The only eternal things are the qualities you develop as a person.

In chapter 1 we discovered that when we make our primary measure of success the feedback and accolades of other people, we will probably always feel like a failure. Likewise, you must recognize that you don't have anything to prove to anyone.

You're a worthy person already. Believe that, and act on your belief, and you will enter a growth and success cycle that you never dreamed existed.

You Can't Fail

Life is a test no one need fail. Since life is a testing time, you aren't likely to be perfect at everything you try—that wouldn't be much of a test—but neither are you likely to fail at the most important things either. The only way a person can fail is to give up, because there is no such thing as real failure for the person who tries. Of course, making a decision that some specific thing isn't worth the effort and then altering that goal isn't the same as giving up—if it's actually an informed decision and not just quitting.

The world calls for many kinds of skills. Unfortunately, societies have often recognized and valued only certain specific ones. For example, look at the mental area: for decades in the school setting, students who didn't excel at academics often felt like failures. Only in recent years have psychologists pointed out that there are other mental abilities beyond the standard academic one that are of great value in life and in school. One categorization indicates that there are at least six such areas and that everyone excels at one or more of them. Look at these six areas and see if you can determine in which one or two categories your strengths lie.

Academics: the ability to learn and mentally organize new material so as to find meaning in it and then be able to rehearse it back under some type of test situation.

Creativity: the talent of coming up with new ways of looking at material learned, making intuitive leaps beyond the facts and putting things together in new ways.

Decision making: the ability to come to firm conclusions about what's been learned and to make decisions regarding its application in our lives. It may surprise you that this is a skill in itself—since we all make decisions—but if you look around, you'll notice people who have little ability at making wise choices. They can't put things together very well to come up with decisions of lasting significance.

Forecasting: the ability to put together the information and knowledge we have and apply it to the future. Such a skill requires clear thinking and the logic to combine the past and the present with the information at hand so as to speak about the coming day.

Planning: an organizational skill, for the purpose of categorizing the world, laying out a course or direction, and thinking through the implications of making this or that choice.

Communication: a skill that requires clarity of thought and an ability to express feelings and thoughts in such a way that others can understand them.

Someone who is strong in one of these areas might not have any skill at all in another. For example, a person who learns information easily (academic) might not have the ability to tell it to another person (communication) or to apply it in new ways (creativity). Another who may be good at applying what he's learned to his own situations (decision making) may fail at looking ahead and using the past as a predictor (forecasting).

Perhaps you haven't had sufficient experience with some of these areas to recognize for sure where your strong points are, but keep in mind that no one is good at all of these, and we're all pretty good at one or two of them. Knowing this helps us keep our heads high.

The point is not to label yourself a failure just because you aren't as good at any one of these skills as you would like to be. One of the facts most people face is that they aren't always good at the things they want most to be good at. But they're very likely to be good at some things that others envy. If you're not as good as you would like to be in certain things, you still have other strengths.

Conclusion

Self-esteem is critical to success. You have to recognize your own worth to believe that you can achieve. Since God loves you and others love you, you can learn to care about yourself. Feeling you are a worthwhile person isn't egotism. On the contrary, such a view is absolutely vital. Self-worth is reality; you are of worth. Self-image isn't always based on reality because it's your own view of yourself, and if you think of yourself as worthless, your self-image is inaccurate. It must be changed, and it can be. If you can accept your problems as challenges, you will enjoy the thrill of mastering them and will come to feel that you are a person of worth after all. Once you do that, you are on your way and nothing can stop you.

3
TIME MANAGEMENT:
You Can't Manage Time,
but You Can Manage You

Have you noticed that the world is filled with many things that will take up your time? In our culture we have so many choices about how to spend our time that finding things to do is seldom the problem. More often the concern is finding time to do all that we'd like to. But we can't do all things, not even all the worthwhile ones, in one lifetime, so learning to make wise time choices is vital to success and happiness.

People say time is money. We even talk about "spending time" as if a week's allotment of it were a stack of greenbacks. But time is a lot more than money—it's life. The passing of time is the passing of life. And once life passes, it can't be retrieved. We only have one chance at it.

A vital question about your time—and your life—is, "Who decides how it will be spent?" If you leave that decision entirely to the TV, your friends, or society in general, you will not likely accomplish much of what you set out to do. Your time will be consumed by these and other outside forces. Some people have, in effect, turned over control of their time to other people. They make few choices about what they do, but leave those decisions to friends, teachers, parents, and others.

Take Jim for example—a bad example. One Thursday night he got a call from a buddy who wanted to go to a movie. Jim had a lot of studying to do before Monday and knew he didn't really have time for the show, especially since the next night was a school dance he was committed to attend and Saturday he was going skiing on a long-planned outing with his family. But Jim did want to see the film, and he really hadn't learned how to say no to a friend, so he did the easy thing—he went. The trouble was that he had a big history test on Monday, and that was also the last day to turn in extra credit, which he really needed. The extra credit was what he was planning to begin on Thursday night, but when the silver screen beckoned, Jim succumbed.

The next two days were as hectic as expected. By Sunday evening the idea of extra credit had been abandoned, and Jim still hadn't even prepared for the test. He decided he would have to miss a ward youth fireside to study. That made him feel a little guilty since his priest's quorum was in charge and he had helped plan the event, but he knew he had to open that history book. When his mom asked him why he wasn't at the fireside, he snapped at her and said that he didn't have time for everything.

People like Jim are often on edge and upset because their lives seem out of control and they constantly feel pressured. It's true that they aren't in charge of their lives; they've allowed others to control them. You may feel somewhat the same way at times.

There is an alternative to this frustrating way of life. It is to take control of your own life. If you take charge and manage yourself, you will get things done. Setting your own priorities and determining what *you* want to do, such as saying to yourself "Sure I like TV, but I can't spend more than four hours a week watching it," is taking control of yourself, and that's a great feeling.

I won't attempt to tell you how to spend your time. That's up to you—it's your life. But I can help you learn some skills for using your time and your life the way *you* want to.

Time and You: Who Manages Whom?

If the title of this chapter strikes you as odd, take another look at it. In part it means that time passes in the same way for all of us and we're completely unable to make it slow down, speed up, or stop, as much as we might like to at times. Sometimes a particular day, hour, or moment may seem to go slow, such as when the dentist is whirring that horrible sounding drill on your tooth and you're sure you've been groaning under it for an hour or more, but the clock shows only two minutes have gone by.

An hour may seem to go fast, such as the hour before the dental appointment when you're hating the thought of going and you're wishing the phone would ring with the news that the dentist was leaving for a slow trip around the world by kayak and will call you sometime in the next decade. But that hour passes like two minutes, and suddenly you're reclining in that soft, vinyl chair wishing you were anyplace else in the universe, while the dental assistant, hiding a sadistic smile, sharpens up the instruments and wipes the beads of cold sweat from your forehead.

But these views of time, of course, are only your subjective views; in neither of these cases has time actually sped up or slowed down at all. The clock has kept right on ticking at the same predictable rate, and your wishes haven't changed a thing. In fact, if you could have controlled it, you would have speeded up the dentist's chair time and slowed down the previous hour. But it seemed just the opposite. Time just doesn't let itself be managed very well, does it.

Sometimes we hear advice about managing time by making lists and schedules of the thing we need to do. This is good advice, but not because it actually allows us to manage time. Does writing our plans on a piece of paper actually control time? No, time will pass just the same whether or not we make schedules, whether we're awake or asleep, whether we're hard at work dusting the chandelier in the main banquet room of the family yacht or hard at rest lolling on the upper deck sipping a dram of nectar.

What we're doing when we make schedules, goals, and plans is not managing time, but trying to manage ourselves. This distinction isn't just semantics; it's a significantly more realistic way to think of time than the managing-time view. Think of it like this: "Though I can't manage time, I can manage me. I can determine that I will spend an hour with this and twenty-seven minutes with that. I can take charge of myself and make me do what I tell me." And that's one of the big secrets to success. Since you can't create or discover more time, your only choice is to utilize effectively the time you have—by managing yourself.

This matter requires a decision. When your decision is to take charge, you take a giant step toward accomplishing those things you want to do and creating growth and independence in yourself. With this attitude, you stand a good chance of feeling satisfaction at the end of each day, because you'll be able to look back and know that you have accomplished much of what was important to you.

People who don't recognize this concept about managing themselves rather than managing time are often looking for more time and using strange phrases like, "I just don't have the time." They haven't realized that they have exactly as much time as anyone else, twenty-four hours in each day, and that they'll never find more of it. Unfortunately, time doesn't come in magic vials hidden by leprechauns in hollow logs. Everyone knows this already, but some people run their lives as if they don't know it because they're always looking for more time. People with this looking-for-time view are trying to control the ocean rather than the ship. But, alas, they will never master time; they will have to manage themselves.

Have you noticed that we generally seem to have time for those things we really want to do, and that we reserve the handy "no-time" excuse for those things we don't enjoy very much, like vacuuming the lint balls from under the bed and writing the Christmas thank-you notes for 1983. For those events and activities that interest us, we "find" time by organizing and planning and sometimes by moving less interesting things out of the way. For the things we enjoy, we become pretty good self-managers. If we could learn to do this more often—especially for those activities of greatest importance in our lives, whether we enjoy them or not—we would become more effective self-managers. And many successful people have learned to do just that. How do these people who have learned the skills and made the decision for effective self-management differ from the rest of us? In several ways.

They start early, set their own deadlines, and control interruptions. They plan their weeks, their days, and their hours. These people may not work any harder than anyone else, but they get more done because their work is organized and focused and they know how to see a task to the end. They're the type about whom people say, "I don't see how they do so much. Don't they ever sleep?" Of course they sleep, but when they're awake, they're fully awake and in charge of themselves. They identify their main tasks in life, and they work in systematic ways toward completing these tasks.

"I just don't have enough time," some people say.

"Neither do I," thinks one who understands how to manage self. "I just do my best with what I have."

Planning Your Week: Looking Seven Days Ahead

When we decide to take charge of our lives, there are many points at which we could start. We could look at where we want to be and what we want to have accomplished by next month or next year or ten years from now. In a later chapter, we will look at just how to set those long-term goals, but for now we'll start a little closer to the present. If we can first learn to manage one week at a time, one day at a time, and one hour at a time, we'll be off to a good start in managing ourselves. Let's start with the week.

Corporations often hire consultants to help their employees better use their time on the job. But before recommendations can be made about where improvement is needed, a determination about how time is currently being spent is necessary. Therefore, the consultant will sometimes peek over a person's shoulder every day for a week, recording exactly what is done in each quarter-hour segment of the day.

The results of these observations are always surprising to the person being watched. Often executives who pride themselves on efficiency will learn from such a study that they just re-shuffle papers on their desks for two hours a day or spend eight hours a week searching for information in files that aren't properly organized. When such things are pointed out, procedures can be changed so that for the same amount of time used and energy expended more work gets done. Such simple time studies have saved corporations millions of work hours and billions of dollars.

You can learn about your own time use without hiring someone to watch you all week. You can watch yourself. The time study just described has three phases: observation, analysis, and planning.

During phase one, observation, record how you spend every hour. On a sheet of paper, mark a column for each day of this week. Down the left margin, write the hours of the day from the time you wake up to the time you go to bed. Then, as well as you can remember, fill in how you spent last week—if it was a typical week—or at least the last few days. If you find it too hard to remember what you've done over the past week and want to be a little more accurate, you can start today to keep your record for the coming week.

After you take away time for school and sleep, these observations will help you determine where the rest of your week goes. Of the 168 hours in a week, sleep may take about 60 hours and if you're a student, class time and travel time to and from school takes 40 hours, leaving 68 hours. From that, subtract grooming, eating, family time, and church, and you may have somewhere between 20 to 40 hours left. These are your discretionary hours, the hours you have the most control over. Observe them closely, because how they are spent will determine to a large extent whether you achieve success in those things you want to do.

Now that you've observed how your time is used, you are ready to begin phase two, the analysis stage, where you decide if the way your time is spent is how you want it to be spent. General guidelines are hard to give here, but if you find that you're spending too much time with TV, recreation, talking on the phone, or a part-time job, you've perhaps discovered part of the problem.

Note that I'm not saying you shouldn't watch TV, talk on the phone, enjoy recreational activities, or hold a part-time job. How you spend your life isn't up to me, and whether you want to change the way you use your time is your choice, but now that you know where your time goes, you're prepared to make some decisions. Ask yourself a few questions: Are you satisfied with your time use? Are you putting in enough time on your most important activities to make real progress? Do you know what the most important activities are for you at this point in your life? Are there areas you want to spend more time on—or less?

In the observation phase, Jan kept track of her time for a week and came up with some interesting facts. After subtracting school time, sleep, meals, grooming, household chores, church, and family home evening, she found that she had 36 hours left. In the week she recorded, which was a typical one for her, she listed the following items: homework, 10; dating and recreation, 5; talking to friends, 4; TV, 10; shopping, 1; looking for a summer job, 2; and tasks too short to count, lost, or unidentified, 4.

Next, in phase two, Jan analyzed this information. Most categories seemed fine, but she was surprised about two areas. She was startled to learn that she had spent ten full hours in front of the TV, since she couldn't remember much of what she had seen. Also surprising was the fact that she had spent only ten hours on her homework. This was about half as much time as she would have predicted, and it was no more than she spent on TV. To hear Jan talk, she was always doing homework, but her own time record didn't show that to be true.

Although Jan was a good student, she often felt like she wasn't fully prepared in class, and she sometimes had to rush through homework assignments because she was out of time and hadn't set proper priorities. She had always felt that she was a hardworking student, but her time study showed a lot less effort than she had perceived. With this new information, and with Jan's admission that she wasn't completely satisfied with the ways things were going, she realized she had a decision to make. Should she leave things as they were, or should she make some changes in her time use to improve her school preparation? She really could use some extra study time. Because Jan took the time to observe and analyze her use of time, she saw an opportunity to be better prepared and to improve her grades and her knowledge. She decided to make some changes.

We've all made similar resolutions, I'm sure. Sometimes, though, at this point, we make a big mistake. We assume that all we need to do is decide to change. But Jan had already had experience with these empty resolutions. She knew that a resolution without a plan is like a car without a motor; neither one will go anyplace except downhill. So she entered phase three, the planning stage, wherein she had to decide *how* to change her time use.

Jan knew that taking more time for homework meant she had to take time from something else; she couldn't create any new time. Looking at each category, Jan didn't want to cut into sleep or family time. She also felt that the time she spent on conversations with friends, dating, and recreation was not excessive and decided not to decrease it if she didn't have to. But she did decide to cut her TV time in half by being more selective in what she watched, and she decided to allot the extra time to her homework. From that point on, there would be no more indiscriminate television watching for her. Each week, she would lay out a schedule of TV shows she would watch, listing only those programs that really interested her.

Jan's next step was to plan a new master schedule for her week. Previously she had fitted her homework in around TV and other evening events. Now she decided that the opposite should be the case. Identifying that her main task at this point in her life was her schooling, she determined that TV would have to be worked in around the demands of her homework. So Jan scheduled her evening study time a little tighter. Four nights a week, Jan would do homework from 7:00 to 10:00. Breaks could be taken as needed, but this time block was to be work time. Such a schedule left Friday night and all day Saturday and Sunday open for other activities, but Jan wisely considered some of that time as additional homework time in case it was needed. That way, even if one or more of her week nights met with interference, she could make up the time. Her general goal was to be done with all homework no later than noon on Saturday, so as to leave the rest of the weekend free. Jan also set aside the hour each weekday afternoon from 4:00 to 5:00 for homework. Getting an early start before dinner made her feel more in control. She especially liked laying out her work, seeing what she had to do, and getting organized for the evening's work.

With these simple decisions—which weren't any real sacrifice but did require determination to stick to the new schedule—Jan's next week went much better. Her homework time was increased by fifty percent, she felt better about her class preparation, and she didn't feel she had missed a thing on TV that she really wanted to see. In three easy steps—observation, analysis, and planning—she had taken control of her time.

Notice that cutting down on TV wasn't enough. Jan had to decide how to use her newly available time. Cutting out time wasters alone wouldn't have helped. The void had to be filled, or Jan would likely have fallen back into the old patterns or found new ways to waste time.

Assuming you've studied your time use and decided you want to get more done in the future than in the past, your next step is to make plans for the coming week so that you can spend more time at what you want to do. Of course, you needn't be afraid to alter your schedule if other important things come up. You're the boss, after all.

Planning Tomorrow: Making Lists

Now that we've looked at planning the week, let's move to dealing with each day in a more specific way. Since you need to know how you're already spending your time before you can decide to change, take a few minutes and list by the hour or half hour what you did yesterday. You should be able to be more specific in looking over one day than you were in looking back over the week. Then look at your list to see if it describes how you would spend the day if you could live it over again. If yesterday wasn't typical for some reason, use another day that was more typical. Then consider these questions: What would you change about your time use on a given day? Is there anything about it that surprises you? Do you find that you're spending more time on nonessentials than you want to?

We've all heard the recommendation to plan our day by just listing those things we want to do, and this is pretty good advice. Making lists is the simplest and most easily applied form of goal setting. A good list provides you with a simple map of your day, giving you a much better sense of direction and keeping you on track.

It's easy. Before going to bed tonight, just list the things you want to do tomorrow. That alone gives some organization to your day, and besides, crossing things off as you do them the next day is satisfying and motivating. Sometimes, though, simple lists have a way of getting out of hand. They get longer and longer each day and soon you may have a list that is just impossible to complete. Then you've defeated your purpose in making the list, because frustration sets in and makes you feel like a failure. Here are possible ways around that problem.

After making your list, ask yourself: "If I only get two or three of these things done, which ones will they be?" By marking a number one beside your highest priority, a number two beside the second, and a number three beside the third, then even if you don't get everything on the list finished, you will have done the most important things and still feel good about your accomplishment.

Or you might prefer this approach: after you've made your list of things to do, take a sheet of paper and divide it into three columns. Then categorize those things you MUST do, those you HOPE to do, and those you will do if you GET TIME. If you work on the "Must's" first, you shouldn't feel like a failure if you don't get to the "Hope's" and the "Get time's." If each day you're getting through a few of your "Must's," you're still doing very well.

Writing your list is the easy part; now you must follow it. When you want to do something that isn't on the list, ask yourself if the new activity is better than what's listed. Maybe it is—especially if the new item is something important that came up after you made up your list—and if so, go ahead and do it; if not, stop and go back to the list.

None of this makes you a slave to the list; you can alter it at any time by deciding that the new activity is more important than those you listed. But you must be careful about it; if you're always finding new things to do other than those you wrote down, a problem exists. You're possibly not being realistic in what you plan, or you're expecting or demanding too much of yourself, or you're not exerting the self-discipline necessary to stick to the list. In the latter case, writing the list is a waste of time and can produce useless guilt, leaving you worse off than before. If you don't plan to do it, don't write it down. If you write it down, try your best to do it. Your list is your manager.

If everything on your list doesn't get done, decide what to carry over until the next day. Don't be discouraged by not finishing everything. Remember that you probably accomplished more than you would have without the list, and there's always tomorrow.

Jan found that by listing her plans and setting priorities on them, she felt much better about what she got done. Sometimes she had to change her goals a little. For example, assignments in class often varied the amount of homework she had to do at night. But she stayed flexible and this was no problem. In fact, Jan noticed that deciding which class to work on was easier with her new approach. Her tendency to do the easier but less important work first was altered as she looked at her assignments in terms of what was the most important.

Planning the Next Hour: Concentration

Hours are harder to deal with than days or weeks. If you were surprised at how you spent your week or your day, you will probably be more surprised at how you spend an hour. Try a small time-use study. When you sit down to a task that needs concentrated time, such as homework, look at the clock. Then note each interruption and daydream, and keep a record of how many minutes you deviate from your task. Even very good students will often find they are spending far less time actually studying than they had thought. They're sitting at the desk, but their efficiency isn't very good.

As a teenager I took this idea to a more scientific level and hooked up a clock on my desk to an on-off switch, creating a homemade stopwatch. Setting the hands to twelve o'clock, I would turn on the switch when I sat down to study. At each phone call, trip to the refrigerator, daydream, or distraction of any kind, no matter how brief, I switched off the clock until I started studying again.

At first I was shocked to find that at the end of four hours of "study," my clock only showed something like 1:43. In four hours I had actually studied an hour and forty-three minutes. My efficiency and concentration were terrible. But by knowing this fact I was able to work on keeping my mind on the task.

Such improved concentration not only made me a more efficient learner, but also allowed me to get more done in less time. After all, since I was getting less than two hours of actual study out of my four hours of sitting at the desk, if I could just concentrate for two productive hours, I could get through my work faster and have time left for other things. This was a very worthwhile and motivating insight for me.

You needn't actually time yourself to benefit from this approach. Even without a stopwatch, if you pay attention to how often your mind wanders and then force it not to, you will concentrate much better. Effective use of a short period of time, such as an hour, is largely a matter of concentration. If you find that you can't keep your mind on your work for an hour, set a goal of doing so for the next ten minutes. Tell yourself that unless the smoke alarm goes off you will absolutely not look up from your book for ten minutes. Set a timer if you wish, but don't let anything interrupt your concentration for ten minutes. By working in these short segments, you will accomplish a great deal.

At the end of that time, take a break, stretch, get a drink, and walk around. Then come back for ten more minutes, but don't start again until you're certain that you're ready to stick to the full time. You'll find that you can handle ten minutes at a time, and shortly, you will be able to do fifteen, then twenty, then thirty minutes at a time. You will have taken control of your time and become much more efficient.

Since other things often come to mind while you're studying, you might want to keep paper and pencil nearby to jot down those things you think of, so that you can take care of them later. Just don't let them stop you now. Finish your ten minutes first, then come back to your notes.

Jan was a pretty good student, but she found that her mind wandered. While reading her biology assignment, she would suddenly find herself thinking of what her English teacher had said about Hawthorne's writing style or of her upcoming date on Friday night. She tried the ten-minute method and found that, in a few weeks, she was able to stay with her task until finished. She had trained herself to concentrate, and it made a big difference in her comprehension ability.

Activity Isn't Always Accomplishment

Keeping busy is easier than being productive. As mentioned before, time-use specialists have identified a phenomenon in the business world called "desk straightening." This is observed in some executives who spend a good deal of time busily organizing and reorganizing their work and the papers on their desks. They're planners and organizers, but not doers. Such people are not accomplishing nearly as much as they might; they're spending too much time moving things around and getting ready to work. But since this all takes effort, energy, and thought, these people feel that they've accomplished a lot at the end of the day, and they're just as tired as if they had.

The desk-straightening attitude is hard to give up because it really is satisfying to have everything ready. And though some amount of planning and organizing is worthwhile in helping things go better when a person gets down to work, in itself it isn't real accomplishment. No matter how much time we put in, if we aren't progressing on our tasks and getting results, we're not accomplishing.

A student with the keep-busy attitude may feel cheated when a project he or she has spent hours on gets a poor grade. But in schoolwork, as well as in many other things in life, the pay isn't by the hour—it's only the finished project that counts. It's been said that working hard isn't enough; we have to work smart.

There's another danger with the keep-busy attitude. A student can easily get the feeling that he's dumb because he's spending a lot of time at his studies but not succeeding very well. The real problem may be that he does not know how to study in an efficient way. Increasing the study time seems to have little value for such a student and, in fact, may make the problem worse. Since he's now increased his study time and is still not successful, he decides he is a failure at school. And in school matters, failure often comes across as stupid, which harms his self-image in other things. If you're in such a situation and feel you are in need of a review of study skills, even after you've tried the ten-minute approach above, see a teacher or counselor or buy a study-skills book for extra help.

Jan noticed that she spent quite a bit of time getting ready to do her homework. She laid out pencils and paper, opened books, and straightened her room so there would be no distractions. She made schedules, charts, and lists of how she would use her time, but she delayed getting down to work. By noticing this, she was able to kick the over-planning habit and get down to work more quickly. She found that her greatest motivator was the feeling accomplishment gave her.

How much desk straightening do you do? A certain amount of getting ready, planning, and organizing is essential, but not when they impede or replace real work. If you find yourself postponing the actual work, that's a danger signal.

Handling Interruptions

We've talked of the progress you can make by taking charge, as if you actually had control over all things. But, of course, there are others in the world—family, friends, and others—whom you can't always control. The best of plans are going to be interrupted, especially in a family setting. Brothers and sisters, parents, friends, and Mr. Bell's wonderful but sometimes irritating invention are all going to disturb your work. How can these interruptions be handled?

The first step is a mental adjustment. Just accepting the fact that such things will happen will help a lot in your handling of them. That's a simple solution to many things. Just plan on the inevitable, and such interruptions will bother you less.

But you can do more than that; you can also manage these intrusions to a great extent. Step two is to get the help of your family. They will understand if you say you'd like to be uninterrupted during your study time. They can take phone messages for you, and they can hold off coming to ask you if you happen to know where the extra vacuum-cleaner bags are.

Of course, this tighter schedule doesn't mean neglecting family chores or family members. Helping around the house is part of your responsibility, too, and should be scheduled into your week like any other activity. Family members can cut down the interruptions to help you out, but don't lock them out of your life because you want to study. Be sure to have an approachable time. If you don't want to be interrupted for the next hour, fine, but make it clear when you *will* come out of hiding—you'll need a break anyway—and that you'll be glad to spend some time with them when you're finished.

It's important to determine your main task. If you are a student, your main task at this point in your life is likely to be the task of learning. But life doesn't allow us just a single track by any means, and there are other important roles that must not be neglected. We all have several roles and can't afford the luxury of doing only one thing, though I believe that each of us has a main task for different points in our lives. Balance is vital. Don't let your main task become your only one. But don't let other things replace your main task.

One extra caution about family interruptions: little brothers and sisters get excited to tell their older siblings the things that happened to them that day. Please allow them to bother you, unless it is too excessive; then you could ask a parent to restrict them somewhat. But don't cut them out of your life. They need you, and you may be a hero to them. Avoid the mistake in this regard that some young people make. After leaving home for college, a mission, or marriage, many have reported regrets because they didn't spend a little more time with their younger siblings, as pesky as they seemed at the time.

Keep in mind that there are "once only's" in life. These are important things that come up and, although they interrupt our plans and schedules, they need to be done *now* if they are ever to be done. An unexpected visit from a seldom-seen, out-of-town friend is probably a "once only." If the time isn't taken to sit down and talk together now, the chance may not come again for some time. Life brings quite a few of these "once only's." Be wise about them. Be sure they're authentic and not just an excuse to get out of your scheduled work, but take the genuine ones when they come. Some people have been so tied to their schedules that they failed to take advantage of these moments. Later they regretted having missed out and, usually, couldn't even remember what they were so busy with at the time.

Conclusion

Learning to manage self is one of life's most valuable skills, one that some people never learn. The necessity of self-management is clear when we come to realize that time is our most valuable asset and the only one that is totally nonrenewable. Once time goes past, it can't be retrieved. Though we can't manage time—in the sense of slowing it down, speeding it up, or creating more of it—we can learn to manage self.

As you plan and schedule your way through the hours, days, and weeks before you, you will gain a sense of mastery of your life that is very rewarding. Be careful not to interpret all this talk of time use to mean that you must be busy all the time or that there is no room for relaxation. A frantic, hectic life can be unhealthy and is sometimes just a screen for lack of direction.

Work is certainly not the only thing in life. But since it's a necessary thing for most of us and a valuable thing for all of us, effective use of work hours can make us better at our tasks, as well as leave us more time for the other things we want to do. Don't let scheduling and planning become the masters; let them be the tools to make your life better. It's a change only you can make, and a strong decision to manage yourself will do wonders for your future.

4
PROCRASTINATION:
Will the Job
Be Easier Tomorrow?

Procrastination, or the I'll-start-later syndrome, is one of mankind's most common impediments to success. There is simply no place for this vice in the lives of successful people because it's the ultimate evidence that we've let time manage us, rather than vice versa. While psychologists tell us that procrastination is sometimes a symptom of deeper problems, often it's nothing more than a bad habit we've gotten into. In this case it can be overcome and, if we're to be truly successful, must be overcome.

Yet, for many people, delaying things that need to be done has become a way of life. They're constantly running to catch up on those things that should have been started sooner. Someone has suggested that if all the world's procrastinators were summoned and laid end to end, the line would be pretty short—not because there aren't plenty of such people, but because most of them wouldn't show up until next week.

Not only is procrastination common, it's commonly regretted. Most people really want to get over this ailment. How often have we said, "Next time I've got to start sooner," and meant it too. Sounds simple enough, doesn't it? But next time is just like this time, and we're late again.

Procrastinators aren't always lazy people. It isn't that they don't work hard; sometimes they may work harder than other people, since they're notorious for staging those amusing all-night marathons to write school papers due the next day and for frantically puffing through the housecleaning before mom's deadline runs out. Yes, they likely know how to work; that's not the problem. They just don't know how to manage themselves.

The student who waits until the eve of the due date to begin a large assignment, for example, isn't necessarily lazy. Often he just doesn't know any better; he's the type of poor self-manager discussed in chapter 3. He doesn't control his use of the time available to him. With the paper now due tomorrow, the work that could have been spread over several weeks has to be done in one night, and the delay has made the job an overwhelming task. For such a student, it isn't the inability to work but a slow take off that's the problem. When we look under his hood, we find that he doesn't need a bigger engine but just a new starter motor.

There are simple steps to curing procrastination; they are so simple that you probably won't be impressed until you try them. But they really work, and they won't even cause you more effort—they actually seem to cause less.

Since doing a job early is no more difficult—and frequently less difficult—than doing it late, overcoming procrastination is mostly a matter of deciding when to start. The good news is that the sickness of procrastination has a remedy, and like all principles of successful living, the first and most important parts of the cure are the desire and the decision to get well.

If you want to stop procrastinating, then stop procrastinating the decision to stop procrastinating. Decide to stop and mean it. Then the ideas described here will be more than interesting reading; they will be the exact medicine needed to restore you to the healthy road to success.

Sneaking Up On It

Sneaking up on your work is another way of saying "do a little at a time." Here's how it works. Suppose a student has a term paper to write that appears difficult and not too much fun; it needs to be done in two months. Most of us, upon receiving such an assignment, go through a thought process something like this: "Two months is a long time, so I won't worry about it for a couple of weeks. (You know the old saying: Never put off till tomorrow what can be put off till next week.) But I'll surely get started then, and I'll get done on time. I want a good grade on this."

In fact, that's just what Paul thought when he received an assignment in his social-studies class. But those two I'll-worry-about-it-later weeks were soon gone, and he was still saying, "I just don't have time right now, but I'll get to it later. I've still got six whole weeks."

As we might have guessed, five and five-sevenths of the "six whole weeks" had suddenly passed, and the due date was only two days away when Paul ran to the library to scribble some quick notes. The next night he gulped down a few bites of dinner and hurried to his room, where his study desk was littered with his note cards. He moved some of them aside to slide his typewriter into place, placed a piece of paper in the machine, and looked at the first stack of cards.

"I'll just have to skip the first-draft stage," he sighed, "not to mention the second-draft stage. This paper has to be turned in tomorrow or else." As he started on his all-night endurance test, already depressed that his paper had no chance of being very good, he wondered, "When will I ever learn to start sooner?"

Three doors down the street, a different scene was unfolding. In the same class, Hal had received the identical assignment, but his thoughts went like this:

1. "I'd better get started. I'll give it some thought and choose my topic by day after tomorrow."

2. "I'll start my research next Monday by looking up my sources and researching one book per day. That way I can get the main research and note taking done in just a few minutes a day in the library. By doing one book per school day for three weeks, I'll have fifteen sources."

3. "Then I'll start the writing and organizing of the paper and work on that for the next four weeks."

4. "Two days before the paper is due, I'll type the final draft so that the night before it's due I can proofread it one more time and make any corrections needed."

Hal had a realistic and workable plan. Now, the night before the paper was due, he checked it over one more time, corrected two typing errors, bound the pages in a yellow plastic cover, and got a good night's sleep, while down the street, Paul was propping his eyes open with toothpicks and typing his one and only draft.

Is Hal really a better student than Paul is? Actually, they're both concerned and conscientious and they both wanted to do a good job. But comparing Hal's method to Paul's method is like comparing a power saw to a fingernail file when both are trying to saw down a giant redwood tree.

Notice that Hal's plan succeeded because he did the main part of his work by sneaking up on it; he did a little at a time so the job didn't seem too big. He managed his research in thirty minutes a day over fifteen days. That's seven and a half hours, but since those hours were spread out, the task didn't seem hard. Paul, on the other hand, did his research all at once. He waited until the next-to-last night, the librarian had to kick him out of the library at closing time, and the whole process was *work*.

When I was an administrator in the BYU Department of Independent Study, I saw many students begin correspondence courses, which they had up to a year to finish but sometimes put off until it was too late. Many of them would then write in for an extension of time. At the end of the additional six months, some still hadn't finished, not because the work was so hard, but because they just didn't get started on time and didn't keep at the task. Interestingly, most of those who did complete their courses did so in the first four months, rather than in the last months. These were the students who scheduled their work and sneaked up on it by doing a lesson or two a week on a regular basis.

Besides term papers and independent-study courses, there are lots of other jobs that seem to go better when handled a little at a time on a regular schedule. Keeping a room clean and neat has always seemed to me easier if done a little bit every day rather than waiting until mom says, "Does anyone remember if the carpet in here is green or blue?" Keeping a desk cleared, ironing, doing the laundry, and weeding the garden all go better when done in regular, small segments instead of day-long work-a-thons. Book and article writing, for me at least, falls in this category too. In fact, this book is the result of a commitment to work on it daily until finished.

Filing of articles and thoughts for church talks, lessons, and writing projects is a chore that I simply can't stand to do for more than a few minutes at a time. Years ago, before applying the do-a-little-at-a-time idea to the filing task, and while waiting and waiting until I "had time" or felt motivated, I got very little done on this task. But I felt anxious about it, because I really wanted the materials filed.

Finally, after years of good intentions, I decided to file two items every day, a sixty-second job at most. In a few months, the two big boxes of unsorted materials that I had tripped over for years were filed, and the job hadn't seemed like work. Keeping up from that point on was easy.

There are clearly some jobs that don't lend themselves to this approach. If the task is painting a bedroom, to stir the paint, limber up the brushes, throw down the drop cloths, put on painting clothes, open the window, and then take three swipes at the ceiling before cleaning up and putting everything away until tomorrow wouldn't be very efficient. Getting out all your genealogical materials only to spend five minutes on a group sheet seems a bother. Some things, therefore, do require a bigger block of time. But it's surprising how many things can be done with a minimal daily effort. And the best part is that most of these jobs are accomplished *without ever seeming like work*. I suppose I shouldn't admit it, but that aspect is one of the things I like most about this approach.

Becoming Your Own Boss
Many young people feel burdened with the concept that their lives aren't their own, that they are constantly living for their teachers, church leaders, parents, or friends. This feeling overcomes us when we're always late with some assignment, project, or household chore. Dark clouds hang over us because we don't feel quite free. That's when people seem to "get on our backs." And that's when we reply, "All right, all right, I'll do it. I just need a little more time."

This dismal picture can change. You can get ahead of it all. Not with a Mary Poppins magic broom that does all the work, but with another nearly magical idea: make yourself the boss. "I have too many bosses already; that's the problem!" you say. Maybe you'll like another way of saying it: set your own deadlines.

It's really a simple procedure. Suppose you're a student and you stroll into class in the first week of October, carefree and relaxed. You're suddenly brought to attention when Mr. Gillam announces that a term paper with at least fifteen references will be due December 15. If you're typical, you think, "OK, that's over two months away. No problem."

And what happens? Well, typically you never quite find time to do much about that paper during October and November. It's on your mind, gnawing away, but you don't do a thing about it. Then about December 8, your sense of impending doom starts to intensify; by the eleventh, your first rush visit to the library for research is made; by December 13, you're in a state of panic, omitting all other homework; and of course, the night of the fourteenth is a no-sleep session. It rather sounds like Paul's approach, doesn't it?

Somehow, the paper gets done and turned in on time, and you're proud of yourself because you stayed awake all night. You're a survivor who pulled through in the clutch. But you're not very proud of the paper. You hope Mr. Gillam is generous, but you know in your heart you've done about C-minus work. The research is haphazard and incomplete, and the writing reads like the first draft that it is.

But things don't have to be this way. Here's a better approach. Way back in October, when you get the assignment, come home and open your personal planning calendar—just a small date book will do—and you notice a few activities already scheduled for December. On the eighth, let's say, your journal is due in your creative-writing class, and that will be a big project. On the tenth, a Sunday, you're assigned to speak in a seminary-sponsored sacrament meeting, and on the fifth, your brother is coming home from his mission; you'll have to move out of his room, put his stereo back together, and rewax his skis. All of this plus December's Christmas preparations— this will be a busy time, much too busy to try to do a term paper in that period. It would be a disaster.

The way to apply the concept of being your own boss to this situation is simply to decide that you won't turn in the paper on the due date, but on some other date. Since Mr. Gillam won't likely negotiate receiving the paper after his assigned date, it will have to be done before the due date, say November 30.

I know how astonishing it must sound to consider doing the job before it has to be done. But look at the advantages: with the paper out of the way, you'll have time to put the finishing touches on the creative-writing journal, work on the church talk, do some Christmas shopping, and spend time with your brother explaining how his ski got poked through his three-way speaker and other interesting things he'll likely want to know.

You'll have time for all of these events and for the other unpredictables that are certain to come up if you get that paper done early. And think of the psychological power and good feeling you will obtain by setting your own deadline, becoming your own supervisor, and turning in the paper when *you* choose. There's also the secret pleasure of seeing Mr. Gillam's mouth drop open. Of course, if you're afraid your classmates will think you've lost your senses, you can hold the finished paper until the due date, and nobody will know.

Now you look at your November schedule. Let's assume that November is relatively clear. October looks OK. There seems to be no reason you can't finish by November 30 if you really want to. Seven weeks is plenty of time if you get started right away.

Congratulations—with this simple procedure, you've just become your own boss. It's a powerful idea that makes you feel awfully good about yourself, because it starts you on your way to managing your own life.

Planning Backward

You're not finished yet, however. For your deadline to be realized, you need a plan, a schedule. It won't do to leave the paper until the last week of November, so you must make your schedule now, remembering the earlier idea of sneaking up on it by doing a little at a time.

A good approach is to build your schedule in reverse, starting with the November 30 deadline and moving backward. Let's say you decide to leave yourself plenty of time for the final typing, so you schedule it from November 26 to 29. Now, moving back again from that week, you plan a week for the final draft, starting on November 19. Let's assume you're one of those good students who writes three or more drafts, so you leave a week (November 12 to 16) for the second draft and two weeks (October 29 to November 9) for the first one. Three weeks for researching, finding one source per day, will take most of October. Your reverse scheduling brings you up to the current week, meaning you will have to consider possible topics and choose one in the next three or four days. Narrowing down the choices and selecting a topic is often the hardest part, so you'll really have to put your mind to the task to avoid ruining your well-planned schedule.

You've now scheduled your time for success. If you follow that schedule, you will achieve your goal of turning in a decent term paper, and you won't need a last-minute crash session to do so. Of course, you will have to apply the ideas from chapter 3 about planning your weeks, days, and hours to actually get the job done.

These ideas don't do away with the work. A paper of this size is still a tough assignment and will be just as much effort as if you did it the way the procrastinators do. But these methods spread out the work, lessen the load on any given day, and move the mountain a spoonful at a time. They also completely eliminate any last-minute panic—if you maintain your schedule. And if you're delayed by sickness or some other unforeseen difficulty, you can move your due date back a week or more and still get the paper in on Mr. Gillam's date without having to beg for an extra day; just check with your own calendar—you're the boss, aren't you?

Conclusion

Are you ready to try these ideas for overcoming procrastination? Think of the possibilities. The next time mom says "Either clean up this room by Saturday or I'm having it condemned!", why not do so immediately, and perhaps commit to yourself that she won't ever have to remind you again? It would make you the boss, wouldn't it, at least in part? And the surprised look on mom's face ought to be worth something.

What about the next time you have an assignment to get a fireside speaker, decorate for a dance, arrange some refreshments for an activity, buy some gas for the lawn mower? All of these and countless others of our daily tasks lend themselves to early deadlines. Home teaching and visiting teaching can be great experiences when you make the visit by the middle of the month—your deadline—instead of the last day. And think what an early visit communicates to the families you visit: "We wanted to come," instead of "Our supervisor called and reminded us, so we had to come."

Getting started with these ideas takes only two prime ingredients: a healthy determination to run your own life and a decision to start today.

5
GOALS:
Your Road Map
through Life

Now's the time to bring out the old sports analogy. Would it seem silly to play a football game on a field with no end zones or goalposts, just endless yard markers going on for miles in both directions? What would be the point of moving the ball if there were no goal line to cross? Some masochistic types might find enjoyment in going out on the field and bashing each other around for a while, but for most people, interest would wane shortly without some hope of scoring, some feeling of accomplishment.

Why is the offensive team in football so much more elated when they move the ball from the five-yard line into the end zone, compared to moving it from the fifty to the forty-five? Five yards is five yards, isn't it? Yes, but when they've made the *last* five yards, they've accomplished their goal of entering the end zone and putting a score on the board. And this small movement of a funny-shaped, inflated piece of pigskin (it's really cowhide) often makes grown men, even seasoned professionals, jump around deliriously, hug each other, and do somersaults right there under the goalposts.

Goal accomplishment is like that. We react positively to having done what we made plans to do, sometimes when no one else even knows about it, even if the attainment isn't terribly significant in the long run. It's a good feeling to be able to say to ourselves, "I did it. I achieved what I set out to do." It's a growth feeling, a feeling that says we're people in control of our lives.

As tools for helping us take control of and succeed in life, nothing beats a list of realistic goals. Goals differentiate us from those who believe that luck or other outside forces run their lives. Let them think what they wish, but as for our own lives, we know that we are in charge.

Goals Are "Me-Managers"

Goals show us what is possible and how much can be done in a given period of time. By focusing our energies in this way, realistic goals make us stretch and do more than we otherwise could do. Maybe it's because of the desire for success that we discussed in chapter 1, but there's something in most of us that makes us want to do better today than we did yesterday. Meaningful goals have a way of bringing out that desire, so that we work harder and reach higher than we otherwise would.

Goals are "me-managers." They help us give shape to our futures, so that we can determine just where we want to go. Goals are those plans and objectives that take some concerted, organized effort to achieve, as differentiated from our more routine daily or weekly activities. Call it goal setting, life planning, setting your sights, or aiming high; the results are the same: they keep us on course and give us control of our destiny.

As just one example of this power of self-management, think of the value of setting the goal of doing better work in your English class. Suddenly the fact will dawn on you that that's part of your English teacher's goal for you too. Now the two of you can work together. Instead of resenting the assignments you're given, you can appreciate the things you're asked to do because you realize you're a partner in your education. You might even propose extra credit options that interest you and that contribute to your learning. What you previously called "busy work" suddenly becomes more meaningful, and you find yourself putting real effort into the class and working for different, better reasons than before. Now things have subtly changed. The teacher is no longer the boss, in the sense of demanding work that you don't want to do. Instead, you've formed a partnership with a common goal—your success. Be careful, though, that such an approach isn't too much of a shock to your teacher.

The fact is that good goals put you in charge and give you a road map to take you exactly where you want to go. Even better, this map isn't one you buy at a service station; it's one that you create. Diligently following such a map—if it's designed realistically—will take you down the road of your choice. Without such a map, you'll still end up somewhere but it may be a long way from where you want to be.

I've seen many students who keep themselves so busy studying and reading and writing and working and going to class that they never sit down to plan and organize. They are busy, indeed, but in matters such as learning, busy doesn't count. Success in acquiring knowledge is all that counts. Some of these students are not successful because, though they're working hard, their lives aren't focused. They're heading somewhere, but it's not clear where. They haven't taken time to create their own maps.

Goal setting can be defined as a way of looking at consequences. A person looks ahead and decides that in ten years, he prefers consequence A to consequence B. So he sets goals to achieve consequence A. If he doesn't make that choice and set that goal, he may end up with consequence B, which is not the preferred one. Or he may even end up with consequence C or D that he's never even thought of.

For our purposes, we'll consider that goals come in four levels, starting with those farthest in the future.

> Level 1: Eternal
> Level 2: Seven to ten years in the future
> Level 3: Three to five years in the future
> Level 4: One month to several months in the future

Any effort less than a month or so in duration could, of course, also be called a goal, but might more logically be considered part of effective time management (chapter 3).

Look at this list made by Jerry, age 16, showing what he wants to attain at each level.

Level 1: Eternal
    A. Be in the presence of Heavenly Father
    B. Be eternally married
    C. Be worthy of progressing forever

Level 2: Seven to ten years away
    A. Finish college, at least with a BA, maybe an MA
    B. Marry

C. Begin my profession

D. Start buying a home(?)

Level 3: Three to five years away

A. Be worthy and prepared for a mission and ready to go by age nineteen

B. Get a semester or a year of college done before my mission(?)

C. Save enough money to pay for my mission myself

D. Decide on which college to attend, whether to live at home or go out of town—even out of state(?)

E. Decide on a profession—final decision after my mission(?)

F. Improve my track ability and finish my senior year in the state championships

Level 4: One month to several months away

A. Decide on whether to buy a car before my mission; talk to Dad about it

B. Get a job next summer, hopefully one I can work at each summer and perhaps during the school year

C. Improve my running; talk to coach about technique

D. Finish my Eagle Scout rank

E. Save money for the Varsity Scout river trip next summer

F. Put some skis on layaway before winter(?)

G. Get in more skiing this winter

H. Talk to Mr. Higgins about algebra and how to get some extra help with it

I. Read the scriptures regularly

J. Keep up my grades this semester

Jerry's full list was longer, but this is enough to give an idea of the types of things listed. Notice that the goals get more specific as they get closer to the present. Notice, too, that some of them aren't certainties and have question marks after them. That's just fine for now; this is a sign that Jerry is thinking and weighing alternatives. As he thinks more about these matters and gains more experience, many of these questions will take care of themselves, and he will know how to handle the others better.

This is a good point to stop for a moment and write out some of your own goals at each level. Take four sheets of paper, one for each level, and start writing. Don't worry about being precise at this point; just get the ideas flowing. When that's done, you'll be ready to read the following sections about how to improve and finalize what you've written.

Goals Must Be Specific and Measurable

⌈The first law of goals is that an unwritten goal is no goal at⌉ all.⌋It's like a car with no gas tank or a firecracker without a fuse: lots of potential but no power. Usually people don't take long-term plans too seriously when they only mentally commit to them. They often don't even remember the plans for more than a few moments. So any time spent thinking up plans without pencil in hand and paper in front of you will fall under the category of good intentions, but not goal setting. Writing goals is a necessary first step toward committing to do them.

Besides helping us remember and commit, another value of writing down goals is that doing so forces us to become more specific about what we want to do. The best goals are very specific and very measurable. A goal like "Do better in school" isn't very valuable because there's no indication of what needs to be done to achieve it. Therefore, there's no measurement possible. A goal such as "Earn a B+ average this semester" is better. Still better is "Get an A in algebra this term." Being more specific, as in "Get at least ninety-five percent on each French quiz this semester," is the best of all. This goal is so clearly stated that we will know at any time just how close we are to attainment, and that's the ideal way to state a goal.

Desires such as "Become famous," "Be happy," or "Be a better person" are much too general. They aren't goals; they are dreams, wishes, and hopes. They're a good place to start, but because they aren't measurable and don't tell us how to achieve the goal, they aren't going to do us any good unless they're rewritten in specific, measurable terms.

Now that we've learned about making our goals specific, we can notice that some of the things Jerry listed in the previous section could stand some tightening up. Let's look more closely at one of them: letter *I* under Level 4.

Jerry wanted to improve his understanding of the scrip-

tures. He resolved to "Read the scriptures regularly," and wrote
this goal in his journal that night. A week passed before he
thought a second time about his desire, and in that week, he
hadn't read a word in the scriptures.

We know what his problem was, don't we? He, too, figured
out that he wasn't being specific enough. That evening he sat
down to think about how to turn his wish into a real goal, and
these were some of his thoughts: "If I don't read some each day,
I probably won't get the scriptures read. But I'll get bogged
down if I try to do too much at once. So, I ought to read about
one chapter a day. I think I'll start with the New Testament.
Maybe I could get up at 6:20 instead of 6:30 each weekday
morning and read a chapter then. On weekends, I like to sleep
in, but I could read that day's chapter before I eat breakfast. If
for some reason, I'm late and in a hurry on any day, I could read
the chapter before going to bed that night. I'll start tomorrow
morning and not miss a day until I'm done."

With these thoughts in mind, Jerry rewrote his goal to read
the scriptures as: "Set alarm at 6:20 A.M. Read one NT chapter
every morning, starting with the book of Matthew and going
straight through to Revelations. If missed, read before bed that
night. Don't go to sleep until that day's chapter is read."

Jerry immediately went to his bedside table and set his
alarm clock to the new time. He felt good about his commitment and confident that his goal was specific enough to leave
no room for failure. With the relatively small segments of reading planned, he knew he could read the whole New Testament
without feeling the loss of the ten minutes of sleep each morning. In fact, when he got started, he found that he felt better
about the whole day after his early morning scriptural beginning, and this pattern soon became second nature to him. On
those occasions when he was tired and didn't respond to his
alarm on time, he felt the loss throughout the day, and he had
no trouble remembering to read the chapter that night.

Jerry's original goal was nothing more than a dream or a
wish. He wanted to read the scriptures, but he had no plan, no
road map; therefore, nothing happened. His revision was extremely specific and easy for him to determine how he was
progressing on the attainment of his goal.

Now you'll be able to go back to your own goals you wrote a few moments ago and revise them to be more specific.

Thinking Wild

Some goals are simple and clear: "Do calisthenics for fifteen minutes every morning before breakfast." Others are more complex and offer numerous possibilities, such as choices about a career. A problem some people encounter with this type of complex goal setting is that they limit themselves before they really know much about what they're getting into. They say, "I think I'd like to be a doctor." Then they immediately start thinking of all the reasons they can't do it: "School takes too long and costs too much to get through. Doctors have to get up at night to answer calls. I don't like to play golf on Wednesdays." So already they've limited themselves, without even looking into what's actually required to reach the goal. They've made a determination based on superficial rather than meaningful components and haven't investigated seriously before eliminating possibilities. That's poor goal setting. To overcome the tendency to limit yourself before even getting started, try thinking wild—or in other words, brainstorming.

Brainstorming means to sit down with paper and pencil and start listing possibilities. If your goal involves choosing a career, for example, then list all the professions you might possibly want to enter. If a field sounds even a little bit interesting, though you may not know all its facets, write it down. Don't reject anything yet, unless you know for sure you wouldn't want to do it. You're not committing to anything yet; you're just thinking on paper.

Brainstorming isn't limited by logic or reason or common sense. Columbus was thought a lunatic by most people of his day who knew about his crazy idea to reach the East by sailing west. And what about those Wright brothers thinking man could fly with the birds? Surely the man who made a documentary movie of his ski ride down Mt. Everest must have raised a few eyebrows when he first proposed his dream. So, don't limit yourself. Let the creativity flow, and you will come up with a better list.

By brainstorming, Jerry lengthened his list greatly. Let's

look at what he did with just one of his goals, letter *F* under Level 3: "Improve my track ability and finish my senior year in the state championships."

Here is how Jerry "thought wild" about this goal:

A. Investigate moving my specialty from the 440 to the 880
B. Look into relay team work
C. See if cross-country, long-distance work is better for me; ask coach what he thinks
D. Put in more regular practice time, year-round
E. Set up a schedule to run with Jed or Phil so we can motivate and pace each other
F. Look into track coaching as a career; talk to coach about it
G. See about a summer job with the city recreation department, maybe coaching little kids in track
H. Check the times on previous state winners to see what I have to beat
I. See about college scholarships in track
J. Train for the city marathon for next summer

Jerry now has a much better idea of directions he could take with his track interest. He hasn't committed to doing all or any of these new things, but he's broadened his possibilities.

It's time now to look over your earlier goals with an eye to broadening their scope through brainstorming. Don't limit yourself. Take a little time to list all the possibilities you can think of. These few extra moments will be well worth the time; they will give you a much better view of what can be done with your basic goals.

Refining

Here's where we cross off some of those wild ideas you listed when you were brainstorming. Then you were supposed to think wild; now you can be a little more realistic. But that doesn't mean you can't leave plans on your list that may seem a little far-out to those who don't know how determined you are. Goals are to raise your sights, after all. In the refinement stage we will weigh the costs and see what seems of real value to you.

Set your goals aside for a day or two, if possible, then look at them again. Do they still seem like things you truly want to do? Are they worth the time, pressure, or investment? Do you want to accomplish them enough to pay the price? If the goal you've set takes so much time that there is no time left for family, church, friends, recreation, or other pursuits you feel are worthwhile, then maybe it isn't worth the effort. Be cautious about tossing out a goal just because it sounds hard. But remember that there is a cost, a consequence, to all things, and since no one can do everything, don't be afraid to alter your goals. It's all right to decide that you don't want to be a doctor because you remember that the sight of a popsicle causes you to gag because the stick reminds you of a tongue depressor.

Since one of the purposes of goal setting is to keep us focused and prevent us from starting over every week, we wouldn't want to throw away goals on the spur of the moment. On the other hand, we needn't become a slave to anything—especially something we aren't excited about. If, after careful thought, you simply don't think you want to do some of the things you've listed, discard them. Remember not to demand too much of yourself. Goals help us grow; they do not vault us immediately to perfection. They are meant to make our lives more organized and easy and are not meant to burden us or make us feel guilty for not doing more.

Don't agonize too much if you find yourself wanting to do more than is humanly possible. Wisdom dictates that you probably can't be a neurosurgeon, a jockey, a skywriter, and a plumber all in one lifetime. Wanting to do many things is a sign of a creative mind curiously exploring the possibilities, but you can't do all things if you're going to be any good at them. So you need to be as realistic as you can.

You may find that some of your goals are contradictory. If you listed that you want to graduate from college at age twenty-three and also that you want to return from a mission and travel twice around the world by the same age, you might have a problem with the time frame. Eliminate those goals that just can't work, and then, if necessary, change the time frame. When Jerry looked at his "Thinking Wild" list, he crossed off items *B, C,* and *J* because he felt that they were contradictory to his basic track interests and skills; to try them would detract from what he was best at.

In the next few days, cross the things off your list you feel are not in your best interest. You needn't be in a hurry to do this and may want to ask your parents or others for their advice. If in doubt, leave the item on the list for now. The elimination of good ideas is hard to do, but life is a continual selection process, and we have to get used to the idea that we can't do everything.

Caution: It may seem silly to list goals during "Thinking Wild" just to cross them off again during "Refinement," but resist the temptation to skip or combine these steps. Your list will be much better because of the process of brainstorming, and some of those ideas will almost certainly remain on your final list. Without that step, you wouldn't have come up with some of your more creative ideas.

Short-, Intermediate-, and Long-term Goals

Careers, college degrees (Levels 2 or 3), and eternal marriage (Level 1) are examples of the faraway destination points on your map. They are those long-term goals that you want most in life.

But long-term goals, by themselves, don't seem to be enough. It's necessary to have short-range and intermediate-range goals that contribute to the long-term ones, that tell us which turn to take and which highway to follow as we head toward that distant point. One reason why New Year's resolutions are generally in bad repute is because they are usually large, life-changing commitments without any supporting framework for success; they're bound to fail.

A football team that has only long-term goals (winning the game or making a touchdown on every possession) is not likely to succeed. Sometimes the goal of gaining a few yards, or even a few inches, to get the first down is absolutely vital. Putting together those short-term goals can eventually result in the long-term goal: the touchdown and the win.

Yet I've talked to students who want to be doctors and who have no interest in anatomy class, prospective engineers who don't keep up in math and science, and future novelists who don't like to write. These people haven't analyzed themselves and their prospective fields. They've never discovered what they will have to do in the *short term* to reach their long-range goals. They only smell the pie bubbling in the oven and don't realize the time spent picking, washing, peeling, coring, and cutting the apples.

Such people are living, therefore, in a dream world of wishes, not goals. Writing down short- and medium-range supporting goals would help them see what's required to get to the long-range desire. Only at that point can they decide if it's all worth it after all.

It would do little good, for example, for a student to set a long-term goal of becoming a doctor, but have no short-term goal of getting a good grade in high-school biology each term. Without that preparation (the short-term goal), college classes (the intermediate-term goal) might be more difficult or impossible to enter or complete. In that case, the career (the long-term goal) might be completely unattainable.

Since medicine is a field requiring a careful sequence of preparation, let's use it to further illustrate this point. Barbara listed the following goals:

Long-Range Goal: Becoming a pediatrician

Supporting Intermediate-range Goals:

1. After talking to a school counselor, choose the best classes for my last two years in high school
2. Finish the year with an overall GPA of 3.5 or better, sufficient to assure me entrance into a good university
3. Check on university entrance exams and inquire about how to prepare for them
4. Save two thousand dollars for college by the time I graduate from high school
5. Check on scholarships

Supporting Short-range Goals:

1. Finish this semester's biology term paper early—on *my* schedule—and earn at least a B+ on it
2. Do extra-credit work in algebra to improve my grade and my understanding
3. Save fifty dollars this month for my college fund

It should be obvious how these goals are essential contributors to the long-term goal. In fact, without them, the long-term goal will likely be impossible. With them, and with additional ones added over the next several years, it will almost take care of itself.

You mustn't become discouraged if you don't manage all of your short-term goals. Setting a goal of getting ninety percent on a paper and coming up with eighty-five percent isn't cause for depression. Goals are to help you grow, not to discourage you. After all, without that goal, you might have gotten seventy percent. (This assumes that setting the goal caused you to study harder. If that's not the case, why set the goal in the first place?) Even *failing* a quiz isn't the end of the world, although if you fail too many of them in a particular subject, there comes a time to reevaluate whether you really want a career in that field.

Now, let's give special consideration to Level 4 goals. Some of them are short, simple, and clear and may not require any supporting goals. Others definitely do require support, even though they may only take a month or two to complete. Remember Hal and Paul from chapter 4 with their different approaches to their term papers? They both had the same Level 4 goals, that of getting their papers in and getting good grades, but Hal was the only one with short-range plans: when to start, how much to do each day, and when he wanted to finish. Paul made no such plans.

When we come to *very* short-range goals, such as "I will study for my biology test for the next hour," keep in mind that this type of goal is an extension of the concepts in chapter 3 on using time wisely. Nevertheless, this is still a form of goal setting. The short-range goals can be very helpful in building your self-confidence, because they show you that you can accomplish something right here and now, if you set your mind to it. Often the difference in the good student and the poor student lies in small attainments in self-discipline. Little things add up to big things and lives can be changed in small steps.

Now, back to work. You are now prepared to go back to your list of goals and write some supporting goals beneath them. These intermediate- and short-term goals need to be carefully thought out, as they are the foundation stones of the house you are going to live your life in. By listing the short- and intermediate-range goals, it becomes very clear what is required to attain the long-term one. This is the time to give realistic consideration to whether you are serious about that lofty plan. If that goal is still worth the cost to you, go for it. If not, drop or modify it.

Conclusion

Appropriate goals help you manage you, give you something to shoot for, and keep your priorities straight. Accomplishing a few of them also seems to build confidence and increase feelings of self-esteem. To be able to say "I set a goal and I made it" is a great feeling. Future accomplishment becomes easier with each successful attainment.

Goals take you above the daily grind, give you purpose, and lift your sights so you can see what is, or can be, ahead. They provide a map, your own special one, to keep you on the path you've chosen, giving you direction and putting *you* in charge. They are, in fact, an indispensable tool for achievement and success.

If you've tried some of these ideas now, you have started to feel the power of mature control of your own life. This control isn't for the purpose of defiance or to prove something to others, but is valuable because we all have to be responsible for what we do with our lives. Positive growth-oriented goal attainment is one of the chief means of feeling good about yourself, and once you feel good about yourself, there is no end to the good you can do in the world. Accomplishment takes work, but you can do it, and you'll like how you feel when you're directing your own life.

Success results when we have three things: time, planning, and effort. As for time, you have as much as anyone else. Goals give you the planning and direction. You'll need to supply the effort. What you make of your life will be up to you—no one else—and proper, strong decisions at this point in your life are vital. Are you ready to try these ideas? *My* goal for *you* is that you will sit down and, following the suggestions I've given, create some goals you would like to attain, and then that you will work like crazy to make them happen.

6
PERSISTENCE:
Stick to the Task

You've written out your goals, and you've made a commitment to achieve them. But, after the enthusiasm fades, what keeps you going? Now comes the time for the real work.

If there's a single trait that distinguishes successful people from others, it's persistence. People who succeed have learned to stick to the job. Through all those times when they'd rather do other things, when they're tired and don't even want to look at their task, they manage the energy and dedication to keep at it. They know that nearly every long-term destination has some mud to slog through before the higher ground is reached. Not every task along the way is fun, even when it contributes to our desired end. In fact, sometimes muddling through the short-term goals is the farthest thing from fun.

Mike had taken violin lessons since he was eight years old, and he loved the instrument. His goal of becoming a member of the city symphony was coming closer to reality all the time, and there was little reason to doubt that he would reach his goal. Hard work had moved him up to first chair in the first violin section in the youth symphony, and he loved performing with them. Solo performances at church and other places made him nervous, but he still enjoyed them a lot. He even liked his weekly lessons and the thrill of learning from a master teacher. Much of his practice time was spent on familiar pieces he had come to appreciate. But in spite of all these aspects of the violin that he liked, the many hours of practice were often tedious and just plain hard work. Getting past the short-term goals is often tough. That's where persistence comes in.

The goal of being a psychologist might seem far away when you've spent four hours in the smelly animal lab trying to get those incredibly dense rats to learn their mazes. Throwing the touchdown pass in the homecoming game might be pretty thrilling, but the tiresome routine of practicing that throw, over and over, day after day, isn't likely to be very thrilling at all.

But, though the fog drifts in and lowers the visibility for many of us, persisters manage to keep their goals in view. Somehow they're able to keep the telescope focused on that dim objective, thereby finding the strength to force themselves through the musical scales, the rat mazes, or the scrimmages. They may not like everything they have to do to get there, but they have a clear, powerful vision of what they want in the future—so they persist. It's important that you, too, become a persister and keep your vision clear.

Keeping Yourself Motivated

If you want good grades in school because dad will pay five thousand dollars for each A, that may be ample motivation for you to succeed. But many goals, especially the short-term supporting ones, will have no such obvious external motivation.

Self-motivation is a major key to making goals work. Some goals have a great deal of intrinsic value to you. That is, they seem worth achieving in their own right. Expecting no immediate reward, you still feel they are worth working on for the way they make you feel. Since an intrinsic reward means that no outside compensation is required or expected, this is probably the ideal motivator.

Although all of your goals have some value to you—otherwise you wouldn't be working on them—certain of them may not seem to have enough intrinsic or extrinsic value to keep you going over the long haul. They may promise you things you want, but the rewards seem too far away, too obscured in the fog of the future, for them to motivate you to keep working on them.

Let's take the familiar example of the term paper. You may sincerely want to finish the paper because of the happiness of having it completed (an internal reward) or because you want to learn about the subject (another internal reward), but these may not be enough. The amount of work involved to do the kind of job you'd like to do might outweigh the relief you expect to feel and the knowledge you expect to gain. Besides that, the good grade hoped for (an external reward) may not seem important to you right now, since report cards are so far away. Therefore, neither internal nor external motivations are sufficient to get you moving. In that case, you have a problem. Unless you can come up with some good reason to do the job, some compelling motivator, you will surely fail. Let's talk about how you can supply your own motivation when you need an extra boost to finish a task.

To begin with, a little soul-searching might be in order. It's often helpful to ask yourself why you wanted to achieve the goal. The answer to that may tell you something. If you want to do a super term paper for the compliments you might receive from friends, or for other shallow reasons, you can now reevaluate if it's really worth the effort. Be sure your true motive is a valid one, one that will sustain you when the going gets tough. If, after this analysis, you still feel that your reasons for wanting to achieve the goal are good, it's time to supply yourself with a motivation for getting the task done. First, let's consider external rewards.

You can design a personalized compensation, such as a day off from working on the paper when you finish the first draft, or a chocolate sundae, or a trip to Bermuda—whatever works for you. Small rewards planned along the way will generally motivate you better than one large reward at the end of your goal. These small remunerations provide something to work for, make life interesting, and relieve the sense of drudgery we may otherwise develop by driving ourselves without a break.

We all perform better if we're working for something specific. Dangling a carrot in front of your own nose may seem a little silly, but it works. If you don't like carrots, find something else. Maybe time off for a couple of video games, a candy bar, an extra hour's sleep, some reading in a good book, or a ten-minute break will personalize the reward for you.

Another approach is to remind yourself of the internal reward that's probably hiding somewhere in your mind. If you can intensify the memory of why this goal is important, you have increased the internal reward and you might not need the carrot. One method is to sit back and imagine yourself having completed the goal. Imaging—creating a strong mental image—is what it's called. Actually, imaging is just controlled daydreaming, and it's simple.

It's easy to close your eyes and imagine yourself succeeding at the task. Visualize yourself on the day you walk up to the desk and place your excellent paper in the teacher's hands, or the day the A grades are handed out, or your first day on the job as you begin the career you are preparing for. Let your mind's eye see how you want things to be, and let that be your motivator.

Imaging means putting clearly before you that image of yourself doing what you want to, so that your memory is refreshed as to what you are working for and what the goal is all about. Sometimes just a moment of imaging is sufficient to get you going again and bounce you right over the bumpy spots on the road to success. In one way or another, with external or internal rewards, you must find a way to make your goals worth achieving.

Making Work into Play

Work is a bad word to many people, and it's not hard to see why. In our simple, black-and-white way of thinking as children, we learned that work was at one end of the activity spectrum and play at the other. Since play was fun, and mother's work assignments sometimes kept us from that fun, work seemed difficult and not enjoyable. Play meant ease and freedom; by comparison, work was drudgery and slavery. We grew up, therefore, with the concept that play was desirable and work wasn't.

Of course, some play was very hard work indeed, but we still called it play if it was something we chose to do and enjoyed doing—at least it beat doing the dishes or cleaning our rooms. Surely mountain climbing, for example, is a great deal of work: it requires extreme physical and mental exertion. Yet mountain climbing is still considered play, hobby, or sport by the people who engage in it. Other enjoyable events also take great effort: chess, football, sailing, river running, and a hard tennis set are anything but restful. Even the initial preparation and practice to learn them properly would be considered real work.

It's clear that the standard childhood idea that work requires energy and is hard, while play is relaxing and easy, isn't quite true. In fact, some people work very hard at their play—much harder, in some cases, than they work at their work.

Then, if effort isn't a distinguishing feature, how does work differ from play? First, one basic distinction is that play implies the freedom to choose how we spend our time. Work has traditionally included freedom of choice. Play, on the other hand, has meant those things that we prefer to do when we don't have to work. Even if the play is more difficult and demanding than what we call work, play is still optional, and that's its charm.

This point is best illustrated by the fact that what is work for one is play for another. For example, fixing broken cars may be play for someone who tinkers with cars, but work for a full-time mechanic. Similarly, a person who loves skiing enough to get a job as an instructor may find that she no longer spends her spare time on the slopes. The activity that used to be play has now become work; it became less fun when it was required. Freedom of choice seems to be a factor in what we call play.

A second distinction between play and work is that the activities we call play are generally intrinsically rewarding to us. They often involve a challenge, and since the mental reward of meeting that challenge is fun—often more fun than the activity itself—we enjoy the experience. For instance, lounging in the water is pleasant. Propelling oneself through it by swimming may be even more fun. But lengthen the distance or increase the speed too much, and swimming becomes work. Yet most of us like to exert ourselves to some degree. We work at swimming a few laps and still call it play. Why? Because there's a good feeling of accomplishment to have swum five laps in a certain amount of time. No one would deny that it's work, but the challenge is met, and that's satisfying.

Since scaling a cliff, keeping a sailplane in the air, playing a musical instrument, or hitting a home run are not easy, there must be more to play than just ease and relaxation. We label play as fun because we are free to choose and because we find rewards in meeting a given challenge. Play becomes work when we *have* to do it, and when the rewards are no longer meaningful. But the opposite is also true: work can often be made into play.

By saying that we can turn work into play, I don't mean to imply that all work can be lighthearted. Some work is anything but fun. But we can make work more like play by remembering the two main qualities that endear us to play, namely, that we are free to choose it and that it rewards us in some way. If you can discover the rewards of the work you have to do, so that you would choose it yourself as part of attaining a greater goal, the work will seem easier and have more value to you. After all, since you are your own boss, I want you to do those things that you yourself choose. An immature approach wastes that concept on lesser freedoms, which means doing anything desired at the moment, while maturity knows that there are greater freedoms; they are those freedoms that come with the attainment of worthwhile goals. Choosing to work hard to gain greater future freedom is a mature use of the power of choice.

The way to real freedom is not to leave out the hard things, but to make them into play by finding their rewards. Then your work becomes play and you actually play all the time, though others think you are working. You are doing the tasks they call work, but since you feel rewarded by those tasks and choose to do them, they are play to you. The people whose work is so rewarding to them that even if they had no need for the money they would continue on in their present jobs are some of the happiest people around. Their work isn't drudgery because they're not working just for the external rewards, but for the internal benefits they find in their tasks.

When you have a job that you call "busy work," work that seems to have no purpose, see if you can discover some reason for the task. Jennie is a good example. For years, she resented her piano teacher continuing to require her to practice the scales. Jennie had learned most of them years before, and she saw absolutely no reason to continue playing them; they were so boring. Then one day, while watching TV, she saw a concert pianist who was describing how he practiced scales. Jennie decided there must be some value to scales after all.

Discerning this new value didn't suddenly make playing the scales a great deal of fun for her, but the drudgery was somewhat reduced. When Jennie came to realize that the scales could contribute to her goal of playing well, and that, if she were the music teacher, she would require them of her students, she learned to hate scales less and benefit from them more.

If you can convince yourself that the paper you're working on, the test you're preparing to take, the scales you're practicing, or the book you're assigned to read have interest and value because they contribute to your future goals, then they will take on more of the qualities of play. They will be rewarding, not because they became easier, but because you now see value in them and because they will eventually increase your freedom to do what you want in life.

If you can't convince yourself that the job has value, see if someone else can. A polite, private request of a teacher to explain the value of a certain assignment may tell you a lot. (However, if the explanation isn't convincing, remember that the matter may be out of the individual teacher's control; she may be merely following a required teaching guide.) If, after this explanation, you still aren't convinced that the work is helping you, consider doing a related, additional project that will be more meaningful to you, thus showing the teacher that you are interested in taking responsibility for your own growth.

The best forms of play and the best kinds of work have identical features: freedom of choice and internal rewards that give them meaning.

Be Careful of Shortcuts

We all like to find ways to make our work easier. There's nothing wrong with that. In fact, much of this book is designed to do that very thing. A shortcut that makes the task easier, but still leaves you accomplishing the essential parts of the job, is a reasonable and intelligent thing. Such a shortcut allows you to do more in the same time period.

One way to get more done is to blend, or piggyback, your work. If your history teacher assigns a paper, for instance, ask your English instructor if you can use it for credit in English class too. Often the answer will be no, but it's worth asking. Be sure that both teachers approve in advance, and note that turning it in as an assignment in both classes *without* prior clearance will likely be thought of as cheating. But if you can convince both teachers in advance that you are applying useful skills from each subject, you have blended two things, not only gaining information about the history topic but, in addition, getting extra writing improvement through the English teacher's help. Serendipity is another word for it, meaning to find value in unexpected places. Keep your eyes open for ways of getting double value out of your efforts. This is a great type of shortcut.

However, there is another kind of shortcut that is cheating. It's a symptom of the worst kind of laziness, the kind that says, "Just let me get the job done, I don't care how." Let me outline two forms of this behavior.

Actual cheating is the most obvious. A student who copies his work from someone else, "borrows" answers in a test, or gets someone else to do part of a job for him without crediting that person, is a thief.

There are, of course, numerous excuses given for cheating: "Everyone does it," "This assignment is so stupid; it's not worth the time," "I'm out of time," "I really know how to do this work already, so there's no reason I can't just copy instead of going through the whole exercise," and "Just this once." All of these are rationalizations, and none of them holds up in the light of day.

What a cheater doesn't know or care about at the time is that, in his effort to fool the teacher, he ends up hurting himself. And he shortchanges himself in more ways than one. By taking the easy but crooked route, it's obvious that the cheater loses out on knowledge because he doesn't learn the material well, but he also does himself even more significant harm. He wounds his self-image, his view of himself. He might think he's very clever to have found a way around the system, but I'm afraid there is deep damage done. In developing a self-image of himself as a sneak and a swindler, even if that image is a subconscious one, he has hurt his chances at success, because very likely he won't expect as much from himself in the future. I couldn't prove that this lowered expectation occurs, but I believe it does.

Finding easier ways *through* things isn't likely cheating; finding ways *around* them may be. By trying to avoid, ignore, or steal from others the central tasks of a job, a person has hurt his own potential by developing a habit of seeking the easy way around—not through—work. Such an approach automatically limits what he will attempt in life. If he doesn't see an easy way to do something, he won't usually try very hard, thereby limiting his own future.

Besides the extensive internal damages, cheating hardly ever goes undetected by others. Teachers might not be able to prove cheating, so they don't always mention it to a student. But once they suspect it, their view of that person is colored from that point on. Cheating is the kind of false shortcut that turns out to be a much longer route. Cheating is a form of lying: indirectly telling the teacher, the boss, or a parent that you put in work and accomplished something you really didn't do. It is a sin against others as well as against yourself. And even if it were true, which it isn't, that everyone else cheats, repentance is needed before further harm is done.

There's a second kind of shortcut, which doesn't have the obvious immoral overtones of cheating, but is nevertheless harmful to growth. It's the view that says, "Let me slop along at my present level; it's good enough." I've seen it often in classes, especially at the university level. On entering college, many students, even those who did well in high school, are unprepared for the difficult work load they encounter. As some of them struggle to turn in work that is acceptable, I've seen various reactions to teacher criticism of their work. More than one has told me that their high-school English grades prove that they are already good writers, implying that I should just let them remain at their current level.

Some talk as if they don't have time to check all the spelling, punctuation, and structure problems in their writing. (They usually say they don't *have* time, but what they mean is that managing their time to get the job done right isn't worth their trouble.) What they're implying is that they have attained all the knowledge they want on the subject and they don't want to be forced into a higher level. They've "learned how to write" in high school, and they don't want to learn any more.

This mental set—when a little is known, no more is needed—is a hard one to combat, because we're all a little lazy in certain things. When Jean went to work at a fast foods restaurant, she was shown several key duties on the first day by some of the other employees. They helped her get started so that she could function in the job. Within a few days, Jean felt that she knew her job. When the manager set up training sessions with her and the other new employees, Jean found it hard to accept that she needed any further instruction. Only when she paid careful attention did she find that, while she knew the main tasks, she didn't know the finer points that would make her a valuable employee. Fortunately, Jean concluded that she wanted to become a great employee and eventually know everything that the manager knew. She put her mind to learning all the details—even to unlearning some things she had learned incorrectly in her first days on the job.

It's easy to think that we know all we need to know in a given area. It's harder to decide that we want to know all we can know. But the difference in these two attitudes distinguishes the plodder from the champion. The hard truth is that much of what we're asked to do in life is often a little repetitious. However, although the material is not brand new to us, it can still give us further proficiency and deeper knowledge.

It may seem silly to an infantry recruit to be required to learn to disassemble and assemble his rifle with a blindfold on. He's already learned how the gun works, and how to take it apart and put it together again in a few seconds. But why in the dark? Later he finds himself in a field situation where his rifle has jammed and, guess what? That's right, the sun is on the other side of the world at the moment. His "silly" blindfold practices now seem a little more useful.

I'm not naive enough to think that all school assignments or chores around the house are that clearly applicable. Some chores really don't seem to have much purpose. In some of those cases, even asking a teacher or parent to help you see why a given task is important might not help. The bathroom sink might have to be scrubbed, regardless of whether anything is learned from the experience.

In sports, in music, in household chores, in most anything we might do, there are ways to take shortcuts that harm the final outcome. Sometimes there's a fine line between a real shortcut that helps you do the job more easily and a hurtful one that gets you out of the job. An outsider might not always be able to tell which kind of shortcut you are taking, but *you* will know—if you make it a practice to be honest with yourself.

Expect Crises

If the Red Cross announced after a natural disaster that there were no supplies on hand because they didn't know the dam was going to break or the tornado touch down, we would think they were a very poor relief organization. Actually, they're a very good relief organization for precisely the reason that, while they don't know *which* dam will give way or *where* a storm is going to hit, they do expect that type of event to happen somewhere, sometime. Their job is to stay ready and to expect the worst.

Life is full of crises, large and small. They effect your life and mine, and like the Red Cross, our job is to expect them and to work them into our plans. I'm not talking about earthquakes, hurricanes, and volcanic eruptions. I'm talking about the small stuff that sometimes turns into big stuff because we didn't plan ahead. If you're absent from class one day but wait too long to get the notes from a friend, and then the friend isn't home the night before the test, you haven't planned well. If you need to go to the library for research, but you leave that visit till the last possible evening and then find there's no family transportation available because you gave no advance notice, you blew it by waiting too long. Getting sick the night before an assignment is due is unpredictable and, therefore, a good excuse. But it isn't a good excuse if the assignment was given weeks earlier. In that case, waiting until the last night is just sloppy planning.

As you've noticed, these unpredictable things do happen. A good planner doesn't play it so close to the line. Plan on crises and give yourself a way out. Expect the unexpected. The fact is that many crises can be managed in advance. Last minute problems and minor crises affect us most when we don't leave ourselves enough time; then the least interruption throws us off schedule. It's essentially a matter of managing yourself so as to leave time for the things that will, inevitably, come up.

When unexpected things come along to slow you down and ruin your well-planned schedule, don't panic, don't run away, and don't give up—just adapt. Do your best with the situation. Turning in an assignment late is better than not doing the work at all, but don't give some silly excuse. Just say you had a problem, that it won't happen again, and that you will understand if the grade is lower because of lateness.

Some people walk around with the view that life is a turmoil and that plans are not going to work out. They use interruptions and crises, large and small, as excuses. "I couldn't do my assignment last night, Mr. Higgins, because my little sister put my book in the dishwasher," they say. While there are occasional legitimate reasons why we don't get things done, many people overuse them.

It may be true that Jim got behind in his chemistry class because of midterm exams in other classes, but what about all the other kids who worked hard and managed to keep up in all their classes? Jim wants mercy from the teacher, but it's really not fair to the others who got down to work instead of begging for compassion.

While I was the supervisor of the Humanities Advisement Center at BYU, I learned that some students had plenty of excuses for not completing required classes. An exemption procedure existed for those with valid cases of misadvisement or transfer problems. But some students expected to be allowed out of requirements on the basis of such reasons as "I didn't ever take this class as a freshman. Surely you won't hold me to it now that I'm a senior," or "I need to graduate *now*," or "I didn't know about the requirement."

While one exemption per graduate was considered the maximum, some students routinely requested three or four. Such people left the impression that they weren't willing to follow the requirements everyone else had to follow, but that they should be exempted just because they asked. "There are no exceptions to the rule that everyone thinks he's an exception to the rule," seemed to be the adage they were proving to me.

Making excuses is a bad habit. Some people always have a handy excuse for their failures. But excuses lower their credibility in the eyes of others and weaken their own self-esteem. It's harmful mental laziness. Many employers, parents, and teachers have no interest in listening to excuses. They just want to see the task done. If not on time, then as soon as possible, but no excuses please. A university teacher I once had always said, "No excuses, Ron. Next time, if you want to feel better, do better."

Review Your Progress

Sitting down with yourself for a weekly self-evaluation is essential to progressing toward your goals. Get out your written goals, and see how many are accomplished now. Checking off those things that are done will make you feel like you're getting someplace. Some of your short-term goals might be fully completed each week, and though the long-range goals will take longer, the weekly review will make your progress clear. Checking up on what you've done in this way reminds you where you're headed and keeps the fog cleared.

The weekly planning session can be thought of as a chance to adjust and reset your course. Each week you will be in a better position to see exactly where you want to go and how close you are. Consider this a time for revisions. You will almost certainly revise some of your supporting goals and occasionally your long-term ones. Now is the time to evaluate whether your time frame is realistic. If you find that you didn't achieve as much as you wanted to in the last week, you will have to decide whether it's because your goals were set too high or whether you're just not working hard enough. Be honest, but be careful not to demand more than is sensible.

People who use this approach to self-evaluation get to know themselves better. If they don't get everything done that they had hoped for, they learn from their mistakes and keep going. They thereby change their bad habits into productive ones and eventually succeed. Although they seldom accomplish everything they want to do, they still succeed because they get so much more done than they would have without this clear analysis of their work habits.

Conclusion

It's relatively easy to set goals and make plans. The hard part is to carry them out, to stick with the task when the going gets tough. Goal setting without persistence equals failure. It's imperative to find ways to keep your nose to the grindstone. This doesn't mean you can't make a rational decision to change, drop, or improve a goal—you're the boss—and it doesn't mean that you don't need breaks from it all at times. But you don't just quit when things get rough, as they occasionally will.

7
TEAMWORK:
There's Strength in Numbers

We need not, and should not, try to go through this world alone. Independence is our goal, but like almost any other principle, it can be taken to the extreme. When a person becomes his own boss to the point of having no interest in the ideas, examples, and lives of others, he is missing out on a great deal. While this book emphasizes taking control of your own life, it's clear that removing yourself from the help of others is going too far.

So much that we do affects others; so much that they do affects us. Humans are social creatures. Wisdom dictates that we take advantage of that fact by learning all we can from our fellow beings. Making your own decisions and taking the responsibility for your own life are the ultimate goals, but it would be shortsighted not to take help along the way from whatever *proper* source is available. And you can get a great deal of help from peers and selected adults—including parents.

One of the best ways to benefit from the ideas of others is to think in terms of becoming part of a team. The concerted effort of a team, a group working for the same cause, is much greater than what an individual can muster. If you can put together a support group of people working for your success, you can gain a great deal from what they have to offer.

Peers and Parents

There's something powerful that happens when the right people work together. *Synergism* is the word for it. It means that the result of their combined action is greater than the sum of the individual efforts. It's like having each of three people drop two dollars into a hat, then reaching in and finding seven dollars; or like having three people, each of whom can lift a hundred pounds, surround a four-hundred pound refrigerator and walk away with it. Four people, each spending an hour on a task, will often accomplish more than one person working six or seven hours.

It's not really magic. It's just synergism, and although it doesn't always occur, when the right combination of people come together, it can be a powerful thing. When two or more close workers aim at the same goal, synergism can propel them far beyond where they individually could have gone. In tapping into this power, teamwork is vital. There are two kinds of teams: visible and invisible. Let's discuss the visible type first.

Although study groups aren't for everyone, they're a good example of how teamwork helps. Tom and Randy decided to form a small study group of students from their sociology class to prepare together for an upcoming midterm exam. They decided to invite no more than two others to join them, and they discussed who would be best. At last, they decided on Eric and Marie, both of whom were invited and accepted the offer. The test was to cover four chapters, so each student took one of the chapters to review. Each was to prepare typed notes on his or her section and come to the next meeting prepared to orally review the chapter and hand out copies of the notes to the other members. All four students had read the material previously as it was covered in class, so they had a pretty good understanding of the information. By working as a team, each student had only to make a careful review of his or her assigned chapter.

The result was a good example of synergism because, for a given amount of work on the part of each person, more was achieved. The total study time was reduced, yet each team member still got a thorough review of all the material. Had the group not existed, each student would have had to review each chapter in depth, and this would have taken more time. An added benefit of working as a team was the opportunity to gain insights and clarifications from one another on unclear points.

A study team, therefore, can be a wonderful help, but you should be aware of the following cautions:

1. If you decide to try a study team, be careful in your selection of participants. Choose those who will contribute and not

just come along for the social interaction. Obviously, if your group is too social and insists on meeting over pizza and talking for an hour or two before getting down to work, or doesn't come prepared, you may end up further behind than studying on your own. A safe start is to begin with just one partner. If that works out, the two of you can discuss whether or not to add others.

2. Avoid those who will leech off of the group's brain power. Each team member must pull his own weight, because a study group really isn't an easy way out. It isn't meant to be less work than studying on your own. It's just more likely to help you learn the material well. Because of the time necessary to bring people together and get down to work, working with a group can be harder and more time-consuming than going it alone.

3. Be cautious about committing to anything at first. If the study group is presented to the others as a permanent, year-long group before it is tested, dropping out may be difficult if it doesn't work out well. It's better in the beginning to commit to just one study session at a time.

When you form a study group, you will find many ways to help one another. Perhaps someone will ask you to read over a term paper before it's turned in, and you may ask for help on your math assignment. Such reciprocal help is excellent and needs to be limited by only two things: your time and the rules of what constitutes improper assistance.

If Eric has you do part of the research on his paper or write part of it for him, you have crossed the line into dishonesty. There is only a limited amount you can do for someone else in the way of schoolwork without its being called cheating. The teacher has to be the final judge of this, but be sure to ask first, especially if you are doing more than looking for typing errors and making general comments about clarity and structure. The writing and research must be entirely Eric's.

Study groups are the most common form of visible teams—now for the invisible one. Such a team is formed out of parents, teachers, and other significant adults. But this group will never meet and will probably not even know the team exists. This team exists only in your mind; that's why I call it invisible. Though this team never meets together, you can still approach

any of them for help at any time. Therefore, this team can still
be a great help in much of what you have to accomplish. Sometimes these significant adults in your life can give specific, tech-
nical help in those areas of their expertise, which might include
such things as math, science, music, athletic skills, or many
other specialties.

How strange it is that we often fail to call on these adults
around us who are interested in our lives, especially when they
are generally so anxious to help. Many students have struggled
through first-year foreign language assignments without ever
asking help of a parent who speaks the language. The same may
be true for any of several other subjects. Some young people
object to asking help of adults, especially parents. "I thought the
goal was independence," they say. But a mature view recog-
nizes that it isn't a weakness to ask for help when needed. Once
we've proven our independence we can forget about proving
anything further and just get on with life. Parents and other
adults can then be seen as equals and their assistance accepted.

There comes a point in growing up when we realize that we
are no longer dependent on parental help and that we would
somehow survive even without it. This self-assurance gives us a
greater freedom to accept help once in a while. We mustn't be
too proud to ask.

Other adults on your invisible team might include teachers,
neighbors, and church leaders. A teacher from a previous year
might be willing to look at some of your more difficult assignments, as long as it's clear that you aren't asking for more help
than is proper and that the job is still your own. Other adults of
your acquaintance could also be good sources of help in
specific fields. A sociology paper might be improved a great
deal from the insights of some of your neighbors: a police officer, a social worker, a hot-line volunteer, an attorney, or a
juvenile court official, for example.

Asking these experts a few questions might help you pick
up some learning beyond what the classroom or textbook can
give. For perhaps the first time in your life, you will be doing
primary research and going directly to the source, rather than
going to a secondary report in an encyclopedia where someone
else has already summarized the sources for you. You are
thereby taking charge of your own education, which you ulti-

mately have to do if you're to get much out of it. Even if you don't happen to know a specialist right in your neighborhood, you can pick up a phone book and find one. Most of them will be happy to answer some questions. Stay alert to these opportunities to use the experts around you.

In my own case, I can recall several invisible team members from my teenage years. Mr. Rathman was an old man who lived a few houses down the street and who was a retired building contractor. He had a huge shop full of tools and liked to do odd jobs around his place, but he was weak and tired and needed help to get much done. He hired me to take care of his yard and help him with his projects, but the real pay was in the stories he told of his work all over the world, and in the shop skills he taught me. I was fifteen or sixteen years old when he died, and I felt a real loss.

Sergeant Hartshorn was another member of my invisible team from whom I learned a great deal. He was one of the full-time army personnel assigned to our high-school ROTC program in Boise, Idaho. I don't remember much about him as a teacher in the classroom, but because he lived between my house and the school, and his older kids sometimes had his car in the evenings, I often gave him a ride to school basketball games when the ROTC had to be there. It was in those casual conversations in the car that I learned the most from him as he talked of his army experiences and his perspectives in dealing with people.

Others could be listed, both adults and kids my age: ham operators who nurtured my interest in amateur radio, teachers who showed an interest in me in various ways, religious leaders who stood for high moral standards, and relatives and friends. All of these were part of my team and helped me in varying degrees. You can have the same benefits by carefully choosing your own invisible team members.

Before we leave this discussion of teams, there's one additional idea in using your team as a motivator that works especially well with parents. The idea is this: write a contract with them. Let me illustrate with a method of losing weight that has proven successful for many people. Several friends get together; each puts fifty dollars into an envelope. Then each states his goal for weight loss for the next month. At the end of the

month, those who made their goal get their money back, and
these same achievers also divide up the money of those who
didn't make their goal. It may sound silly at first, but it works—
for the obvious reason that there is something substantial to
lose if the goal isn't attained.

The same principle can be applied in your situation, without necessarily using money as the motivator. Suppose you
need to write a book report this weekend, it's now Monday and
you've read only half of the book. Because you are aware that
you must finish reading the book during the week if you are to
have quality time on Saturday for writing the report, you determine to finish the reading by Friday night. A contract with your
parents can help you do this job, and it could read as follows: "I
will finish reading *The Grapes of Wrath* by Friday night so that I
may go to the school dance. If I do not finish, I will stay home
and read until I do." You've simply written a statement of your
intent and given it to someone who acts as your monitor. By
clearly stating to someone else what you plan to do—and what
privilege will be earned by completing your plans or denied by
not completing them—you have really put pressure on yourself
to succeed.

Note that it isn't the parents who demand that you finish the
reading. You're still the boss. But you've added an incentive to
do the job, and you've asked a member of your team—parents,
in this case—to act as your enforcer. This is much more effective than just saying to yourself that you will finish Friday—you
hope—if you get a chance—if all goes well. It's taking one step
toward the concepts of chapter 5 on writing down your goals
and of chapter 6 on rewarding yourself. It's committing to
someone else and asking them to prevent you from getting
your reward unless you achieve your contracted statement.
Now, don't make your parents the bad guys in such a deal. Don't
blame them if you don't make it to the dance. If you don't finish
the job, you will be the one to keep yourself from going: you
made the contract, and you should stick to your word.

You will find this approach somewhat effective even if you
just write the contract and don't show it to someone else. But it
will work better if someone else is involved. Also, note that it
isn't someone else's job to come up with effective motivators
for you—like the dance. That's all up to you.

Ask for Advice

Advice is easy to give and hard to take, but it's somehow easier to take, or at least to consider taking, if we ask for it first. If we ask people what they think of the things we want to do, they're free to express their opinions, and of course, we're free to reject them, but we will very often find an idea or two of value and a new way of looking at things.

Businesses, knowing that some of the best ideas come from outside observers, use consultants to tell them how to improve. We can benefit in the same way by asking people for input. Such invited consultants are a valuable part of any team. Here's how you can use the same principle.

During the process of goal selection, especially on things like careers and other long-term plans, share your leanings with someone. This must be a person that you trust to listen carefully and then to honestly advise you, not just a head-nodder. It may be hard for you to believe, but even your parents might want to give a little advice. As long as you make it clear that you'd like to know what they think, but that these are *your* goals, they'll be flattered that you asked, and you needn't be threatened by hearing their views. Other people who know you well—teachers, church leaders, and others—can also be consulted. Let them know that you really want to hear what they think, but don't mislead them into thinking that you are binding yourself to accept their advice. That's up to you; you're the one asking.

As one special segment of the invisible team, I would recommend finding a few people of the grandparent age. These people have seen a lot of life and have had plenty of time to reflect on the choices they've made and what they might have done differently. When a lady in our ward died recently at the age of seventy-seven, my kids were impressed and surprised to learn from her obituary in the newspaper that she had driven an ambulance in World War II, had held several other interesting jobs, and had once been the ward Relief Society president. Since my kids had only known her as an aged, sick widow, they were surprised that she had ever been anything else. You should seek the wisdom that many of these older people have accumulated, and even if you only pick up one idea from one of them, that idea might change your way of looking at things.

Friends your own age can also give input and will often have excellent observations. But remember that they won't have the big picture of you that your parents may have. Though we often like to think that our friends understand us better than the older generation ever could, it isn't always true. Sometimes our friends know many details about us that parents don't know: what musical group is our favorite, which teachers we like, and maybe even what some of our aspirations are. But our friends may have never seen how we deal with day-to-day problems, what we're like under pressure, and how we treat family members—those basics of dealing with people that say so much about our interests and attitudes. Our parents may know a great deal more about us in those important ways than do our friends.

There's another caution about putting too much stock in the advice of peers. Just as parents sometimes seem to expect too much of us—more than is perhaps reasonable at times—some of our friends may expect too little. Don't let your friends limit you. They may not have the vision to see you as president of the United States, but Abe Lincoln's friends probably couldn't imagine that tall, gangly rail-splitter becoming one of the most loved U.S. presidents of all time. Be careful not to let your friends laugh you out of something, or shame you out of your dreams.

There is some pressure in our culture to aim low, so as not to appear superior to our peers. In Samoa, where I taught for three years at the Church College of Western Samoa, I saw this pressure to an even greater extent. In that society, where age has all the advantages, it is considered presumptuous for young people to seem to be too smart or to want to move ahead too fast. Youth are expected to stay in the background and to avoid the appearance of excelling, if excelling appears to take them above the average of their peers or especially of anyone older. Often students in class would purposely avoid doing good work for this reason. A teacher's praise could embarrass students greatly and sometimes cause them to do poor work from that time on.

Even in the American culture, there is a similar feeling among youth at times. In some peer groups, it is somehow unseemly and haughty to proclaim a desire to be something more than average. Be careful that this downward pressure doesn't lower your sights. Keeping this problem in mind, there is still value in talking over goals with trusted friends. They can help you see alternatives, raise questions, and give you insights into yourself that you haven't perceived.

So far, we've talked of asking for advice as you try to select proper goals. But there's another way to use the help of others that comes *after* you've settled on your goals. Once your goals are in place, share them in some detail with someone who values you. You may not wish to share them all, but share as many as possible. The purpose of sharing is to increase your commitment to accomplish, and sharing really does increase that commitment.

Ideally, the person you share with should be someone who can help evaluate your efforts. Then, to get the maximum help, report your progress to this person periodically. Such sharing of goals is a vital element in their attainment, at least for certain types of goals. One study showed that public declaration of sharing made a vast difference in the results of goal setting.

Students in the study were divided into three groups. The members of group one set the goal of improving their grades on an upcoming test; they were to share their goal publicly. The members of group two also set the goal to improve but were not to announce their intentions. Group three was the control group and didn't set any goals for improvement. When the tests were taken and graded, eighty-six percent of the students in group one—those who set a goal for improvement and shared their plans with others—improved their scores significantly, whereas group two—with the same goal but without communicating that goal to anyone—made no significant improvement. In fact, there was no statistical difference between the scores of group two and those of group three, who set no goals at all. ("Tell It from the Mountain," *Psychology Today,* Oct. 1985.)

Obviously, setting goals isn't always enough. Writing them down, as described in chapter 5, will help immensely and is a way of committing to them. But a vital next step is finding someone you can share them with. Sharing makes you more certain of what you really want and puts a little pressure on you to succeed, just because you told someone you would.

Using Others as Examples

If we become careful observers, we can learn something from just about everyone. Even people who exhibit negative traits can teach us. Often they teach us how *not* to be, but this information can be as instructive as observing how to be. Studying people is a way of putting everyone on our own team.

As young children, we often have role models we want to pattern our lives after. As we get older and become more aware of developing our own individual personalities, we sometimes forget that there is still a great deal to learn from others. We have, in fact, already learned a great deal from many others. At particular points in our lives, though, we take it all for granted. I remember when I first became aware of traits in my parents that were admirable. Not until I came into contact with other adults *without* these good qualities did I notice them in my own parents.

We may not notice that much of what we've learned in growing up may be significant information about how to get along in the world and deal with people—information that's essential for living, enduring, and solving life's problems. Once we've learned it, it somehow seems like we always knew it, or like everyone knows it. Sometimes, we have to get older before we can appreciate what was given us.

Watching people is a great sport and an educational one. In fact, much of what we call wisdom in older people didn't come from formal study but is merely the accumulated observations of their having studied other people for years. But when you observe others, you'll notice more things than you can assimilate. You can't adopt everything you see—even all the good traits. Some good traits even seem to contradict other good traits, and though both are desirable, you're still forced to choose what is right for you.

For instance, Julie's bishop had a great gift of listening. He could just sit back and let people talk at length about their lives: what they were working toward, what troubled them, and how things were going. She admired this style greatly and loved going in to talk with Bishop Scott. He seldom offered any advice, but instead just listened. Sometimes Julie received great insights as she listened to herself talking!

Julie's dad was also a good person to talk to, but in quite

another way. He was sort of an interrogator. When Julie talked with her dad about anything significant, she had to be prepared for probing questions about what she really thought and felt, and what she thought the consequences of her ideas were likely to be. Dad's approach was anything but the relaxing approach of the bishop. Her dad made her look hard at what she was saying, and conversations with him were difficult for Julie. Everything was scrutinized, not in a way that made Julie feel judged or condemned, but in a way that helped her see things in new ways and forced her to think. She couldn't get away with inconsistencies in talking with her dad. He forced her to see herself more clearly.

The point is that Julie saw value in both styles. She sometimes needed one and sometimes the other. She admired both approaches, but as she thought about the style she would like to adopt in her own dealings with others, she saw that the two methods contradicted. Her dad couldn't just lean back, relax, and let her talk, and her bishop couldn't, or wouldn't, probe. Both methods were good, they both worked in their own way, and though Julie liked them both, she felt that they couldn't both be adopted. Julie found that she could combine elements of the two, however. As is often the case, Julie had to create her own approach and couldn't just adopt anyone else's. To make the approach hers, she had to change it to suit her personality.

As another example of contradictory approaches, perhaps one of your friends is a tremendous support in everything you want to do. Another friend questions and critiques you and has ideas of her own. Which is better? Well, very likely, you like both approaches. Some days the first is the type of person you want to be around. At other times, her style seems too subservient and weak, and you want someone who has her own views and will tell you what she really thinks. Neither approach is wrong, and each has its strengths. Which should you be? You'll have to create your own style. Observing people will help you sift through the many traits available to find those you want to work on and incorporate into your own life. Don't be afraid to modify them to fit you, however.

Comparisons

As was pointed out in chapter 2, one of the most harmful

things to your progress is to overdo comparing yourself to others. Your goals are your personal goals; whether they're greater or lesser than someone else's isn't the point. Too much time spent comparing yourself to others will make you discouraged because there is always someone who will seem to do better than you do in certain areas. But does this mean you failed? No, not unless you see life as a competition to be won to prove that you are better than someone else. The point is not to be jealous of others. Let them have their strengths and rejoice with them in their successes, because you will have yours too, though not in identical ways.

But there's another positive kind of comparison, a noncompetitive approach that can be very useful and motivating. This comparison is actually a form of observation, as discussed in the previous section. Through observation and comparison, others can be a gauge for us, an example, a part of our team. By watching what they do, we can better learn what is attainable. It's like having a pacer to run with, someone who keeps us moving better, who makes us aware of how much faster we can go.

By closely watching his buddy Tim as he trained for and broke the school high-jump record, Robert was able to improve his own technique. Tim became Robert's pacer, in a way, to show him what could be done in the high jump, and in the next year, sure enough, he broke Tim's record.

In high school, I had an experience of learning from someone else through friendly comparison. ROTC was important to me in high school. At Boise High School around 1960, the program enrolled a large number of young men. My best friend, Dick Hutchison, and I were both in the program. Dick was always a very sharp cadet. I was tall and gangly and never felt that I looked very good in my uniform, but Dick's shorter frame filled his in a way that made him look like a career soldier. He did well in the classes, in inspections, and in drills, and won cadet of the week at least once, which I never did. I admired Dick and used him as my model.

In the beginning of our junior year, we saw an announcement of the selection process for the new supply sergeant. This position involved some after-school work in the supply room, where uniforms and other materials were disbursed. It was considered a prestige position for a junior—the only chance most of us would have that year at the rank of cadet master sergeant. Inevitably, the supply position would lead to the position of supply officer during the senior year and also to the rank of cadet major, one of the four highest staff positions in the battalion.

The competition was open to any junior who could meet the after-hours requirements. "Let's try out for it, Woods," Dick said. "Why not?" I said with something less than wild enthusiasm. On the appointed day, right after school, we arrived in uniform and found the room filled with several others who were there for the same reason. The numbers made the competition look rather stiff, and I think I might have left had Dick not been staying. We were all taken into a huge instruction hall, stationed several feet apart, and called to attention. There we stood while several intimidating senior officers came by, scrutinizing our uniforms and interrogating us on the material ROTC students were to have learned by this point: general orders, chains of command, military history, tactics, and strategies. Some of these things I knew very well. Others were hazy or totally new, and some questions were obviously designed to confuse.

For many long minutes, these older officers, including the current supply officer, strolled up and down the line trying to get us to make a mistake. Occasionally, they would convene for a moment off to the side and then one of them would approach a cadet and dismiss him, whereupon he would salute and leave the room. One by one, people were being eliminated. An hour went by, and we were still at attention. Many young men had been dismissed, and there were but four or five of us left. I was glad to be in the final cut and to see with a quick sideways glance—when no officer was looking—that Dick was still there too.

I was finding myself more and more amazed that I was still there. I was also beginning to question if the supply-sergeant job was worth it. It was exciting to have made it this far, but it was also a big hassle. With so much time invested, however, I wasn't going to quit now.

After another half hour, something happened that neither Dick nor I could have predicted. There were only three of us left when an officer approached the third young man and dismissed him, leaving only Dick and myself. Now I was really un-comfortable. I had no intention when I entered the competition of ending up challenging my best friend. Of course, when we started, I would have bet that Dick would win, but now I wasn't so sure. The fact that I had lasted this long made me want it more myself, although I wished things had turned out so I wasn't pitted against Dick.

On and on it went. The officers, who by now had asked all the questions they knew at least once, came by again and again to take additional closer looks at us; they were looking for flaws in the polishing of our brass insignia, scuff marks on our shoes, wrinkles in the creases in our pants—all of those little things that matter on the military uniform.

Then one of the officers got the idea to drill us. "Forward, march," he barked. "Column, right." "Right oblique, march." "Column, halt." All the possible commands were given as he marched us around the hall for the next ten minutes, looking for mistakes. Finally we were halted and more questions were asked. It was now late; two hours had passed. Then the officers met for another conference, leaving us standing at attention. At last, the supply officer approached Dick and spoke to him. I couldn't believe my ears when I heard, "Corporal Hutchison, dismissed." The supply officer walked over to me and said, "Congratulations, Corporal Woods. You are our new supply sergeant. At ease." I nearly fell over.

The experience as supply sergeant, and later as supply offi-cer, turned out to be one of the great growth experiences of my youth, and although I never actually asked Dick how he felt about not getting the job, his "Way to go, Woods!" as we left to go home told me that he was as happy for me as I would have been for him. The irony is that I would not likely have attained this job if I hadn't modeled myself after my buddy Dick. I proba-bly would not have even tried out for it without his invitation. How I somehow ended up impressing the officers slightly more than he did that day is still a mystery to me.

It would be false to say there was no competitive adrenalin flowing during activities like the supply-sergeant tryouts. But we must keep in mind that we are actually competing with our-selves, not with anyone else, in the important things in life. We should use others as good examples and models of what can be done, not as competitors that we have to beat down. That way all can win, and none need lose. There may be only one supply-sergeant position, but in the *really* important things, there can be a blue ribbon for everyone.

False Images

We all carry many false images around in our heads. As we grow up, we see only partial pictures of things. A five-year-old child has a certain concept of what a doctor is, but a fifteen-year-old young adult probably ought to have a broader view of the profession. Yet we sometimes make decisions about careers on our earliest impressions of a field.

What, for example, do university professors really do? If I were to tell you that they teach from six to twelve hours, would you think I meant from six to twelve hours *per day?* The fact is that, at large universities at least, they generally spend only from six to twelve hours *a week* in front of classes. So what do they do with the rest of their time? Well, they spend a good deal of time preparing for those classes and recovering from them (correcting papers and tests). They are also generally expected to research and write about subjects in their field, be it chemistry, English literature, or music history. In many large schools, they will not be promoted or even retained if they don't succeed in researching, learning, and publishing. They also serve on campus committees, spend a lot of time in meetings, keep current in their fields, and counsel students. They do, therefore, a great deal more than just teach from six to twelve hours a week. But if a young person thought a college professor is someone who only stands before classes, he might have made a decision about a career that would have been very far off the mark.

What do doctors really do? How much of their time is spent on business-related matters: buying supplies and equipment; hiring nurses and helpers; paying insurance premiums, taxes, rent, or lease charges; filling out forms and doing other paperwork? If our image of doctors is only that of the drama of the brain surgeon that saves the life of a president, we may have a distorted view.

Unfortunately, we all have strange ideas of how things really are. Part of growing up is getting some of those ideas straightened out. Much of our education lies in doing just that. As you work out goals for your future, try to correct and supplement your present images of people and careers. One of the best ways to improve those images is to talk to people about their careers. There are people at church, professionals you have dealings with, and family friends that you encounter with whom you could speak.

Do you really know what your neighbor does? Ask, and you'll usually find people eager to talk about their work. Don't ask about money and income. Unless they volunteer that information, it's none of your business. Do try some of the following questions on them:

- What interests you most about your work?
- What was the most surprising thing about your field when you first entered it?
- What is the best part of your work?
- What is the worst?
- Why would you recommend your profession to others?
- Why would you not?
- To be successful in your work, what kind of traits does a person need?
- What kind of person should not go into your work?
- How did you prepare for your work? How much time did it take: What kind of education was required, or did you learn on the job?
- What is required to stay current with your job?
- If you could change the view the public has about your work, what would you change?
- Are there sufficient openings in your field so that a young person today could reasonably expect to be able to enter it and earn a good living?

This doesn't have to be formal interview, with you reading the questions and writing down answers. It can occur at a ward party or across the backyard fence. Just try to learn from others wherever you can and correct a few of those false images. Put these professionals on your team and learn from them.

Know Yourself

One additional false image we likely carry is the image of ourselves. Since it's impossible for us to see ourselves exactly the way others see us, our image of what we are is always going to be somewhat distorted and never fully accurate. But we still have to try to improve our knowledge of ourselves. The better I know me, the more likely it is that I will succeed. The less I know me, the more likely I will expect things of myself that are unrealistic.

A key element in your success is knowing yourself well enough to know what works for you. You can learn a great deal from others, emulate their best traits and see the kind of person you would like to be. But you must couple these observations with some basic knowledge of who you are and what your individual, unique traits are.

In our youth we often think we are totally unique. We suppose that no one has gone through the things we have or had the feelings we've had. We think we're different from all other generations. Sometimes we also think that, individually, we're different from everyone else in our own generation. Of course, we are unique in some ways, but we all are similar in many ways too. If we insist too much on our own uniqueness, we will miss many opportunities to understand others and ourselves.

Though, as children, we sometimes think we're unique, at other times we don't want to be different at all. At certain ages we try to be inconspicuous by being just like everyone else. Just as any extreme has its problems, this one does too. If we try to blend in too much and be a clone of everyone else, we soon become a mere follower with no thoughts of our own.

The ideal is probably a balance between the two positions, but it requires knowing yourself. This self-knowledge equates with putting *you* on your team too.

Here are some suggestions for getting to know yourself better:

1. Don't fight yourself. Sometimes we spend a lot of time and energy trying to be something we're not. We don't recognize our own strengths and use them, but instead insist on being what some false image of ourselves has told us we should be, or we insist on copying someone else we admire. These views miss the point that we can learn from others' strengths without having to be exactly like them. Consider that the people we try to emulate have likely become the kind of people they are by being themselves and emphasizing their own

strengths. Part of your job is to recognize that you have strengths of your own that you need to capitalize on. There are many ways to succeed, and we won't all go about things the same way. Remember that even when you emulate the good traits of others, you will need to adjust these traits to fit your personality.

2. Find your best methods. If you study well with others, for example, organize a study group—as mentioned earlier—and spend your class preparation time with other students. If you do better alone, however, stay out of such groups. Find the best time of day to work. If you're truly a night person, as most teenagers *think* they are, then you can be productive later in the evening. But the world is also filled with a great number of morning people who are more effective earlier in the day. If you're one of these, but you try to force yourself into the night-person mold to match your peers, your work will be less successful than if you get up early and get started.

Some projects need a lot of heavy concentration and require that you be fresh and alert to do them well. Others are more routine and can perhaps be done even at the end of a long day and still come out fine. As a student I knew the temptation to do all the easy tasks first. You should avoid this temptation. You may end up with a chapter of heavy reading in psychology or physics at 11 P.M., wishing you had done it earlier in the day when your brain was still awake.

3. Decide on your own style. An area where you have to find your own way is in the amount of planning, scheduling, listing, and structuring you need and want in your life. Of course, this whole book is about planning and structuring, but you still need to decide how much energy to put into these processes. Some people seem to manage fine with less conscious planning of their day or their week than others. At least they don't write down their plans in any great detail. Most people, though, benefit from such listing.

If, after you use the ideas in chapter 3, you find that you can achieve the same things without the careful pencil and paper approach, go for it. (I'm talking here about time use planning, not goals; goals *always* have to be written down to be successful.) The point of this suggestion is to remind you that, although you will probably benefit from proper structuring of your life, there is a danger of too much. Structure provides security, and like any form of security, some people take structure to the extreme. They become enslaved to their lists and their schedules. Such an extreme has a cost in terms of spontaneity and true freedom. When you become a slave to anything—even good things—you have lost sight of your goal: taking charge of yourself. You, not your lists, must be in charge.

These ideas remind us that we have to know ourselves and what works for us. This self-knowledge will be a lifelong undertaking, because just as you feel you've learned a certain fact about yourself, you will change. We aren't the same at twenty as at fifteen, and we aren't the same at thirty as at twenty. That's part of what makes life exciting.

Conclusion

Teamwork builds success. If you can work together with the people around you, you will likely do better in many things. However, you're still on your own, still independent, and you will still make the main decisions for your own life, because in spite of all the help others can give, you still have to decide what to do with it.

If you try to go at life alone, you may succeed in some things, but you will likely do less well at others. I've often thought how interesting it is to be on the earth at this particular time with this particular group of people. Think of the strength around you. Why shouldn't we tap into that strength to help one another?

8
PERSPECTIVE:
Don't Demand Too Much

T here's a danger in all this talk about goals and time use and planning and succeeding. It is that some readers may take these concepts too far and demand too much of themselves. Some people are perfectionists by nature. They are not willing to settle for reasonable growth and progress; so they insist on excessive demands on themselves. They want perfection in an imperfect world. Unfortunately, the exacting requirements of this approach often make life miserable for these people and for most people around them.

Goals and schedules are your servants; you mustn't become a slave to them. They sometimes have a devilish way of taking over your life. They can make you feel guilty when you aren't pursuing them vigorously enough. "I don't have time for dinner tonight," "I should be studying," "I'm not progressing fast enough," or "If only I didn't need to sleep." Statements like these are possible evidences that your goals and desire for success are exerting too much control over you.

Remember that the point is to give your life more focus, direction, and meaning by making you the boss. Don't lose that by letting your goals become the boss. Manager, yes; boss, no.

Let your goals prod you, prick your conscience, and guide you, but don't let them run your life. As soon as that happens, you'll become unhappy. Goals have a way, once they get to that point, of never being satisfied. "So you made your goal, huh? Big deal," they seem to be saying. "It probably wasn't a very hard one anyway."

When your goals start talking to you like this, you may have to let them know who's in charge. Change them, junk them, laugh at them. If they get too complex, start over. If they don't work, make new ones. Just be sure to keep yourself in the driver's seat.

Perfection Isn't Possible

Some people push themselves too hard; their drive for perfection makes them unable to tolerate anything less, so they're never happy with themselves for decent accomplishment. They're constantly upset with themselves over something: they didn't achieve a 4.0 GPA, or they made a typo in their thirty-six-page term paper. Instead of remembering how much was learned in the effort of doing the paper and feeling good about their work, or at least being glad to have their paper done, these people are upset because it wasn't perfect. This attitude is extremely destructive to happiness.

We mustn't interpret this as meaning that we needn't try for quality work, but we shouldn't tear ourselves down when we find ourselves falling short of perfection. There never was a book published, a paper written, a movie made, a sports event played, or an opera sung that couldn't be improved; nor is perfection possible in most other things we will do in life. We can only do our best and leave it at that.

When we start to tear ourselves down because we're not perfect, it's best to remember that it's better to aim high and succeed partially than to aim low and succeed fully. Partial accomplishment of difficult, worthy goals *is* success.

Some people constantly feel like failures, and they act as if they're the only ones who ever experience this feeling. However, as mentioned in chapter 2, failure is quite normal. People who are successful in life have often failed at many things before achieving the success for which they're known. These people have learned to call failure by a different name, such as *mistake, stepping stone,* or *learning experience.* They've also learned how to pick up and go on.

Furthermore, one success doesn't lead to another; failure can still come again to one who has succeeded earlier. Numerous sports heroes, entertainers, writers, and business people have found themselves starting over after failing or falling from public acceptance. No one can rest on past successes. The tough reality is that life is a constant challenge.

While some people demand too much of themselves, we

need to mention those at the other end of the scale, the people who feel they can't really accomplish much anyway, so they adopt a position of not trying. They underestimate their potential. If they set goals at all, they aim at easy ones to protect themselves from failure. Of course, such low-level goals do them little good because goals have to make us stretch.

The cure for such people is to set some moderately difficult goals, where at least some effort is needed. Success with these will increase their image of themselves as people who can accomplish. Then harder goals will become possible. These people have to learn to take things a step at a time.

This raises another question: Is it all right to have mediocre goals in certain areas? Is it OK to shoot for a *B* in a class, especially a class that isn't our main interest, or must the goal always be an *A*? How about growing a garden even if all the weeds aren't hoed, or writing poetry when we know we're not Shakespeare?

Is such purposeful imperfection acceptable? I happen to think it is—so long as we don't settle for mediocrity in *all* things. Excellence in an area or two is worth working for, but we needn't eliminate all other areas of interest just because we can't spend the time to accomplish all of them perfectly. We can't do everything.

We've heard many times, "If it's worth doing, it's worth doing well." Actually, that is a false statement when we try to apply it to everything we do. People who do insist on doing everything well usually end up being driven to attain perfection in all things. When in spite of their strivings, they still don't achieve perfection, they're never happy.

If you enjoy playing the piano now and then, but really aren't interested in giving enough time to it to go on the concert circuit, why feel guilty? Enjoy the amount of ability you've developed, and spend the greater portion of your energy on those things of greater interest.

Balance

In a chapter on not demanding too much of yourself, the question of balance needs to be raised. Let's start by asking a hard question. Is it better to strive for a single goal with full devotion, or to work on several things at once? There is no right answer, and there are impressive arguments on both sides. Devoting yourself to one major goal will allow you to give it all your attention and perhaps really master it, but you'll miss out on a lot of other activities you might have been involved in. If, on the other hand, you try to accomplish several things, you'll need to reduce the amount of time each of them is allowed and you may never master any of them, though you may attain an acceptable level in some of them.

If you want to be a figure skater in the next Olympic Games, you will need to spend so many hours training every day that you will have to exclude many other activities. If your goal of getting into the Olympics is attained, then fine. But what if you don't make the Olympic cut? Will your attempt still have been worth the effort? And, even if you do make it, will you someday regret having neglected too many other important areas? Only you can say. We hear success stories about those who made such achievements as obtaining the Olympics after valiant effort; we don't usually hear from those who didn't make it after spending the same number of years trying.

In keeping with the Olympic theme, let's look at two winners from the 1984 summer games. They are both gymnasts and are examples of the single-goal approach. Gold-medal winner Mary Lou Retton didn't finish high school on schedule because of the tremendous training pressures to perfect her skill. Was it worth it? Only she can answer that, but I'm sure the decision wasn't easy.

Peter Vidmar, the LDS gymnast, didn't go on a mission because of the intense training he had committed himself to in his teens. We look at him now as an Olympic winner and see that he's performing a different kind of mission, with the publicity he's giving the LDS life-style. But what if he hadn't won and hadn't attained that fame? Would all of that practice have seemed in vain? Would he have regretted the narrow, single-goal training that eliminated other important things? I don't know, but I'll bet he thought long and hard before committing himself to the single-goal approach.

A similar question is faced by those hoping to enter a competitive professional field such as medicine. Some say they should consider a second-choice major and take classes that will provide them with an alternative career should they not get

accepted into medical training, as more than half of the appli-
cants won't. Other advisors feel that such an approach will
dilute their efforts and keep them from putting their best work
into those requirements necessary for medical school acceptance.

It's the old question of whether or not to put all your eggs in
one basket. Though you may not be a world-class champion in
anything, as most of us aren't, you still face the question of
whether to specialize or generalize, whether to try to do a few
things or many. It's a major question, and I have no answer for
you. Only you, in consultation with parents, church leaders, and
experts in your field of interest can decide the approach that's
best for you. My only admonition is to not make the decision
lightly; be sure to weigh the costs.

Perspective

To avoid demanding excessive amounts of ourselves, it's
sometimes required to say no to others. It's a difficult word to
say in our society. We're raised to be polite, helpful, and willing
to lend a hand. So, when we're asked to help with this or that,
our natural reaction is to want to say yes. And we live in a society
where a good deal is asked of us. We're expected to be good
citizens, friends, parents, spouses, children, and contributors to
the common good.

School expects a lot from us. We're to be good students,
doing our best in each class each day, participating in extra activities such as sports, music, or knowledge bowls. We're to be
good school citizens: serving on committees, decorating for
dances, and supporting sports events, plays, and concerts.

Our church asks a lot. We're to keep all the command-
ments, respond to church calls, pay donations, serve missions,
help with welfare projects, attend meetings, and be aware of
opportunities to serve the needs of others.

Our parents may demand a lot. We're to be good family
members, do chores, perhaps earn money and contribute to
our own support, help our younger brothers and sisters, obey,
and meet the family schedule.

And some of you demand a lot of yourselves. You expect
yourself to do well in all the areas mentioned above plus
achieve in other specific goals of your own. All of these things

may have great value, but the cruel fact is that there is not enough time to do them all perfectly well. In spite of all the lists and schedules we might make, there still won't be enough time. Someone has said, "There's never enough time for everything, so learn to do a little less a little better."

Perspective—stepping back from things to take a broader look—is a way of viewing things in their true importance. It turns out that some activities just don't matter very much in comparison to others. A few can be skipped entirely, and others can wait. Once in a while, just waiting until things take care of themselves in time is a solution. (Don't overdo this one, however. Some matters do have to be done, and for some of them, the sooner the better.)

One way to decide where to spend your time is to ask yourself: What's the worst that could happen if I don't do the activity under consideration? Asking that question will help you identify the consequences, and you will sometimes find that the consequences aren't too painful after all. At those times, we have to relax and recognize that life is a series of choices. We will make mistakes, and we will have some regrets because our perspective isn't always perfect and time is limited. We can only do what our best judgment tells us at the moment. When we're diligent and do our best, we're entitled to remain relaxed about life and to feel at peace about our decisions.

Have To's, Want To's, Neither's

One way to keep from demanding more than is reasonable from yourself is to clear your life of extraneous things. Some of us have very cluttered lives. We're trying to do too many things, constantly running between demands and generally living in a hectic way. This may sound like a normal life for teenagers and for lots of adults, but you know by now how I feel about your being a slave to anything. If hectic is your *choice* of life-style, go for it, but if it's forced on you because you've never taken control, I encourage you to analyze carefully. Being busy is fine; being driven isn't.

One way to simplify and thereby have time for the things you really want to do is to determine which ones can be cut out. We've looked at goal setting as a way of determining what you want to do. A step beyond that is to cut out those activities you don't want to do, but somehow find yourself in a pattern of doing.

As you look at your activities, you will find some things that you do out of duty and others that you do out of interest. Someone has suggested listing them under the categories of *Have to's* and *Want To's.* List under the Have To's those items that you feel you must spend time on at this point in your life. The Want To's list is for those things you don't have to do but really would like to do.

The ideal situation is to end up with identical items on the Have To's and the Want To's lists. Then your days will be spent doing only those activities that you really want to do. The person who goes to school or work because that is exactly what he or she wants to do has combined Have To's and Want To's perfectly. That's one reason why an LDS mission is such a great experience for most people. When they realize that they love what they're doing, that it's really just what they would choose to do (the Want To's), then the mission rules (the Have To's) are little or no burden at all.

At most points in our lives, the overlap between these two categories isn't quite as perfect as that. While I hope you'll have some common items on both lists, it isn't likely that they will all coincide perfectly because we all have some Have To's that we'd rather not have; that's part of life. And most of us have more Want To's than we will have time to handle in one lifetime.

Now that you've made those two lists, a third list is needed: *Neither's.* These are the things you find yourself spending time at, but not because you have to or want to. You've somehow gotten into a pattern of doing them without knowing why. Making such a list forces us to ask: "If I don't *have* to do these things and don't *want* to do them, why do them?"

You'll have to be a little careful here, because there are other people in your life who may expect certain things from you. If you decided, for instance, that you don't have to or want to do assigned household chores, you may find a parent with a different idea. Those items then go back on your Have To's list.

Usually the most interesting part of this whole exercise is to see what you list under Neither's. This is where you can make some big decisions about leaving out those activities that don't interest you, nor are required of you. All you need then is the courage to eliminate them from your life. Sometimes there are peer activities that have been outgrown and no longer enjoyed, but which haven't been broken away from. Unless you feel you have to continue them, perhaps for the good of someone else—in which case they should be on the Have To's list—just put them on your Neither's list and discontinue them.

Don't Worry

Now let's talk about the least productive mental activity any of us ever do—worry. Mark Twain made a comment on the futility of worry. He said, "I have known a great many troubles, most of which never happened." We all have such troubles that never happened. We all worry. What we worry about, and how much we worry, differ greatly, but we all worry. Telling you not to worry might be good advice but impossible to follow. But helping you recognize why you worry and discussing ways to control and channel worries into productive energy might help.

The problem is that worry uses up energy and gets us nowhere. If you have a concern and put yourself into the problem-solving mode, you'll think the matter through and probably come up with a solution. If you stay in the worry mode, you'll just fret about it and spin your wheels. Worry simply gets nothing done. It's akin to guilt, which, as we discussed before, is only useful if it motivates you to do better.

A book like this one can cause worry by inducing the feeling that you should be doing more than you are. Insofar as this feeling causes you to want to do better and to make some concrete plans to do so, fine. But when it causes you to feel guilty and tormented, without helping you do anything productive, this feeling isn't good.

Here's a concrete suggestion for getting a handle on your worries: make a worry list. This means to list those concerns that are currently nagging at you. It sounds dumb, but it works quite well. I make such a list now and then myself, and I inevitably discover three things. First, writing the list gets my worries out in the open and makes me feel better almost immediately. Second, the list is always shorter than I had expected. Right away I become aware that my specific troubles are not as numerous as I had thought. The weight of the world I've been carrying on my shoulders turns out to be light enough to put in a knapsack on my back. And third, besides being fewer in number than I had thought, the individual problems don't seem so bad when I see them on paper. They seem more manageable. When I look at the list, and make a few plans for an item or two on it, I know I'm in control again.

One additional thought about worry. It's imperative to recognize worry for what it really is—fear. Many of us say we fear nothing, but worry is actually low-grade fear. You may have never thought of worry that way, but we don't worry about things we are perfectly confident about, do we? It's when we think we're not quite prepared or don't know what to do next or feel we're not in control that we worry.

With this idea in mind, look at the items on your worry list and try to discover what you are afraid of. What are the bad consequences that you fear? Forcing yourself to identify the fear often makes it less scary and provides a starting point to take care of the problem. Action is alway better than fretting.

The futility of worry is illustrated in the following quote from Reinhold Niebuhr: "O God, give us serenity to accept what cannot be changed, courage to change what should be changed, and wisdom to distinguish the one from the other."

Work and Rest

It's clear that hard work is necessary for worthwhile goal attainment. So work hard, but don't leave your engine in overdrive all the time. Work is a great thing, but it is not the only event in life, and it needs to be balanced with rest and relaxation. Take breaks and vacations—long or short—from your work, and don't feel guilty if you're not always charging ahead.

The American culture still carries a heavy influence from the early puritans, who tended to regard leisure as sinful and wasteful. All of us have grown up with the idea that laziness is bad—which it probably is. Without realizing it, we often carry this a step further and equate laziness with leisure. Therefore, anything that smacks of too much relaxation is regarded with suspicion.

Our culture manages to get around this appearance of laziness by approving of active leisure, such as skiing, hiking, and tennis. Since these require energy, they seem like work and, therefore, are acceptable relaxation. But some "lying around doing nothing" is acceptable too, if that's your style. Resting, relaxing, and recouping aren't laziness whether your style be active or passive leisure. Leisure is good and should be planned into your schedule. Take time off when you need to. Go to bed early one night and get recharged, go to the movies, spend time with family or friends, read a poem, catch a fish, climb a mountain, or play at a hobby—whatever relaxes you.

BYU Professor Stephen Covey uses a fine analogy about the woodcutter who is so busy sawing logs that he has no time to sharpen the saw. The woodcutter is afraid he won't get as much done if he stops sawing long enough to sharpen it. Is he right? Do you think he gets more done with a dull saw than if he took the time to sharpen it? Of course not.

It's also true in your life. Borrowing on Professor Covey's analogy, if you don't take time to sharpen the saw by judicious use of leisure time to refresh and sharpen your mind, you will gradually saw fewer logs. Leisure makes you a better worker when you return; no guilt is necessary over appropriate leisure.

The bad news is that just as work can be overdone, so can leisure. Some people spend a lot of time justifying how they had to have a break, and that's why they haven't done any homework yet this month. Of course, they're fooling themselves. In fact, they've just never learned to work. But that doesn't mean that there aren't times when a break really is the right thing at the moment. You be the judge; just be honest with yourself.

Some people neither learn how to work hard nor play hard. They feel like they must always be busy, and since they never get caught up, they don't feel justified in taking a break. They just sluff along all the time: not working hard, but never taking a real break either. Therefore, their work is always hanging like a dark cloud over their mind. They don't ever finish, and they're never free of the burden. That's no good. It eats up energy and becomes drudgery. Learn to work hard, then take time off for play; don't just sluff along halfheartedly.

Conclusion

Goals and planning are your servants, not your bosses. If

you demand perfection, you're going to be an unhappy person that no one likes to have around. Learn to relax and to enjoy life as you go.

The famous American architect Frank Lloyd Wright told about taking a walk when he was nine years old. He was with his uncle, a no-nonsense type, and they had gone across a snow-covered field. Turning around, his uncle asked him to look at their tracks.

"Notice," said the uncle, "how your tracks wander aimlessly back and forth, over there to the trees, then to the cattle, here to throw sticks. But see how mine go straight to the goal. Never forget this."

Frank Lloyd Wright said he didn't ever forget it, but he got a different lesson out of the incident than what his uncle intended. He said, "I determined right then not to miss most of things in life, as my uncle had."

Work hard, but don't miss out on life.

9
ATTENTION:
Life Is
Now in Session

Numerous signs posted in buildings and on roadsides give information, directions, or warnings. Some of them, such as the following, reach out and grab our attention, causing us to behave differently:

QUIET: RECORDING IN PROGRESS
DANGER: BEWARE OF DOG
THIS EXIT IS ALARMED
BLASTING ZONE
PRACTICE BOMBING RANGE

Putting us on the alert, signs like these make us notice our surroundings and help us conform our behavior to those surroundings. We don't want to cough during a recording session, get bitten by a 150-pound wolfhound, set off an alarm, or get blown up.

I once saw another sign that caused me to think twice about what I was doing with my day. It read:

LIFE IS NOW IN SESSION

If we really accept that message, we will behave differently than if we carry around these kinds of ideas: "If I can just get through today (or this week, or this school year, or high school, or college), then I'll enjoy life." "As soon as I find a girl- or boyfriend (or get married, or have children, or move to Jamaica), then I'll be happy." "When I buy a car (or get a job, or buy a house, or get rich, or retire), then everything will be fine." This kind of thinking makes it sound as if life is something that's coming along later, like the evening train. But, though some people apparently haven't noticed, life is already here, waiting for them at the station.

Happiness Is in the Pursuit

The power of the sign, LIFE IS NOW IN SESSION, is in the emphasis on the word *now*. Some people never seem to get that message and live only for tomorrow. The trouble with that idea is simply that the old saying is really true: Tomorrow never comes. And the reason it never comes is that there is always *another* tomorrow to wait for. The person who pins all his hopes on the future hasn't realized that there will always be something else to wait for, and something after that. Therefore, he will always be waiting for the future to make him happy.

At fifteen he's waiting to get through high school; at twenty, he's waiting to get through college or job training; at twenty-three, to get married and get the big job; at twenty-six, to buy the big house; at thirty-four, to get the big promotion; at thirty-seven, to buy the bigger house; at forty-five, to get the kids through college and on their own; at fifty-two, to have grand-children; at sixty-two, to retire; and on it goes.

It's not that looking forward is bad in itself, but some people are always waiting to get something out of the way so they can start to live. The trouble with that view is that all those things they're moving out of the way—so that they can enjoy life—happen to *be* life.

But, you say, setting goals is taught in this book, and isn't goal setting itself a way of living for tomorrow? Yes, it is, but not to the exclusion of today. Goals aren't just to make us happy at some future point; they're to keep us happy as we go. Goals can certainly make our tomorrows better, but only if we don't forget that life is now in session. It's already started, and it's going on with or without us. If we blink, we'll miss it. What we have to do is enjoy where we now are, no matter how much more we hope tomorrow will bring.

Socrates said, "If the Almighty held in his right hand ever-lasting happiness and in his left hand the pursuit of it, I would choose the left hand." It's the pursuit of happiness that is happiness. We must live as we go. The paddle wheeler is steaming by right now, but some people don't notice because they keep watching for it upriver. Their boat won't come down the river again.

The Thick of Thin Things

Waiting for life to happen in the future tends to make us bored with today, but one characteristic of successful people is that they are never bored, or not for long. That's because they have goals they want to accomplish right now. They take charge of their time and go find something to do that's interesting or valuable to them. They don't wait for tomorrow to solve their woes.

Boredom isn't a matter of not having something interesting to do, nor is it a matter of not having enough work to do. There have been people in solitary confinement who weren't bored. Boredom, instead, is an attitude problem. The bored person is waiting for life to come to him. He hasn't yet decided to reach out and grab it. He wants to be entertained or rewarded or made happy by forces outside himself. While that happens occasionally—when we're just sitting there and something comes along to bring us happiness—mainly happiness is in our own minds, in our own ways of thinking, in our own plans and goals. Nobody can afford to waste a life being bored. There are simply too many great things to do.

Since little kids aren't old enough to take charge of themselves, they sometimes go to their mothers to ask, "Mommy, what can I do?" They're tired of their toys and routine activities, and their siblings or friends aren't available to play. So mother suggests that they clean their room or take a bath, and they suddenly remember they wanted to study their rock collection or sit on the front step. Little kids haven't yet looked at their lives in a systematic way—through time-use planning and goal setting—like you have, so they aren't always self-directed. They have, in effect, an attitude problem. Of course, at their age, no one blames them.

In your case, however, you know that your life is all up to you. You have plenty that you want to do. And if you ever feel bored for a moment, you can always go to your list of goals and find something that needs doing.

Lottery winners and others who come into fabulous wealth overnight are sometimes prone to disaster. They often stop working and change their life-style from one of activity to one of sitting around waiting for the next check to come in, and suddenly they're bored. The very way of life they thought would be so wonderful turns out to be incredibly meaningless. There's no purpose, and nothing to pursue. If they're wise, they will keep on striving for some goal. They may, if they wish, quit their old job—their new money, after all, can sometimes buy new opportunities—but they mustn't just retire from meaningful activity. Otherwise, they become like a ship with a sail but no rudder. Note that the money itself isn't what ruined their lives. It's the attitude that they no longer have a need to work, have goals, or render service, and this attitude leaves them directionless. "Man does not live by bread alone," Jesus said. In part, I think he meant that we need a purpose, a direction.

The real slayer of boredom is having meaningful things to do or think. There's a phrase that describes a busy life: "in the thick of things." There's a modern twist that says, "Don't get caught up in the thick of thin things." This is a way of saying that there is much in the world to occupy us, but much of it is just lightweight froth. Some people seem to spend their time doing only those things. Their lives are busy but meaningless—filled with fluff. And meaningless lives do lead to boredom because they have no depth. People with this problem wake up one morning and wonder where their lives have gone and what life is all about.

Helter-skelter, pell-mell, and willy-nilly are good descriptions of these people's lives. They're very busy, but they're busy with superficial trivialities. Instead of walking a direct path to a destination of their own choosing—as a goal setter is able to do—they're running on a treadmill, getting nowhere. When you pursue meaningful goals of self-improvement and service to others, you won't find boredom a problem.

Urgency Versus Importance

Time-use specialists have categorized our worthwhile activities into two types: urgent and important. They aren't always the same. Sometimes the things that are most urgent aren't very important at all. They need to be done, but in the long run, they don't matter much to our eternity. Hurrying home to see a favorite TV show may be urgent because if you don't get there, you'll miss it. But missing it may not really be very important. In the long run, whether you see it or not doesn't matter.

A leaking water pipe in the basement is also urgent. If I'm

upstairs working on my family history, I'm doing something that's clearly more important in the long run. But if I don't see that the leak is taken care of, I might have big problems. So, in this case, the problem is urgent *and* important. At the moment, the urgent even outweighs the family history. If I don't take care of the water problem, I will just have bigger problems later. But here's the point: if I spend most of my time on *only* the urgent, I may wonder why I got nothing important done in life.

Suppose a football coach is taking his team out of town to play in a championship play-off. It's time to leave but the bus won't start. Obviously the most urgent need at the moment is to find a way to get the team to the play-off site. But is this the most important thing the coach has to do that day? Not likely. It's more important in the long run for the game to be played well, and that's the coach's main job today. If he lets the bus problem disturb his own or his team's mental preparation, he may have sacrificed the important for the urgent. If the team's mental energy is dissipated worrying about the bus rather than concentrating on the opposing linemen, the game may be lost, and the coach will have failed in his most important job of the day— even though he managed to get the team to the playing field on time.

At the end of the season, few will excuse the loss of the game by remembering that it happened on the day the bus broke down. Years later, people won't say, "Boy, remember the time the bus broke down and old Coach Lewis hijacked a Greyhound to get our guys to the Higginsville game—which we lost. What a great coach!" They will simply remember the loss. Therefore, if the coach can let an assistant or a school administrator see to another bus, while he stays with the team and keeps their minds on the game, he has chosen to handle the important and let someone else handle the urgent.

Of course—as in the case of the broken water pipe—sometimes things are both urgent and important. If there is no other administrator present to arrange another bus, then the coach may have no choice but to take care of it himself, even if he has to phone ten parents to bring their station wagons. Even if the team's preparation is harmed by having the coach involved, at the moment there is no choice. He simply must get his team to the game. The urgent has become the important.

There are four ways to combine these terms. Tasks can appear in any of the following combinations:

1. urgent but not important
2. urgent and important
3. not urgent but important
4. not urgent and not important

We've already illustrated the first two of these, with the example of the football coach. If he can get someone else to arrange transportation, the matter, for him, falls under number one. If he must do it himself, it's under number two. Number three is the category for most long-term goal setting. The things we do to prepare for a career are quite important, but they're seldom urgent. They may take years to get done. Unfortunately, because they're not urgent, we tend to procrastinate doing them. That's why we discussed rewards and motivators in chapter 6, so that you could find ways of making some of your goals seem a little more urgent. Otherwise, you may put off the important until too late. As for category four, if a task is not urgent and not important, it's the type of activity we ought to consider not doing at all. If there's no hurry and it doesn't matter anyway, why do it?

Categorizing your activities in terms of urgency and importance is one way of helping you keep in mind the big picture when you set goals and make decisions on how to spend your time. The challenge is then to find ways to work on the important and not let the urgent always take over; if we're not careful, that's just what happens. A student who lets sports, practices, shopping, TV, grooming, dates, or social events—all of which might be urgent at the moment—overwhelm his studies has allowed the urgent to take over the important, and the long-term consequences will be serious.

Life Is a Challenge; Enjoy It

Some people get worn-out and worn-down by life. They get burned-out, frazzled, and tired—not just temporarily, but permanently. That's too bad. It's a great waste, and it's not necessary. Burnout is a result of too much stress over situations in which we have too little control. Well, life is a challenge, always was, and always will be. But it's not out to get you. Life can be coped with.

Obviously, we can't judge the situation or mental state of others. Some people do have huge physical, mental, or emotional problems to overcome. But for *most* of us, attitude is the key. If you take the view that you can succeed, you will likely be able to enjoy the challenges and to cope with the disappointments of life. The worst attitude problems—other than the major issue of low self-esteem that we discussed in chapter 2—are pessimism and cynicism. These are the deadliest known murderers of happiness.

Pessimism—the view that things won't turn out right no matter what, and that reality demands a negative view—is bad enough. But cynicism is even worse. Cynicism adds the element of distrust of others, because it supposes that people only act out of their own selfish interests. This is a fatalistic view of humanity that poisons the cynic, making him unable to act in goodwill with others.

Optimists, on the other hand, can be perfectly realistic. They know that things can go wrong, and that nothing will be quite what was expected. But they take the viewpoint that life in general will turn out all right. They expect the best possible outcome. And if that outcome is less than perfect, it's still close enough that they can enjoy the level of success achieved.

Pessimists think that optimists are naive and go through life with blinders on, not seeing things the way they really are. But I contend that it's possible to really see life and still be optimistic. Certainly there are problems, but life is good. It's all in the attitude, and you can choose the attitude you prefer. You can wear the dark glasses of the pessimist, which filter out the light, or you can put on the often-maligned rose-colored glasses of the optimist, which allow the light of hope and confidence to come through.

The point is that your way of seeing life is critical to how you approach it. We see things as our attitude programs us to see them. Never underestimate the power of attitude, because it is a reflection of the power of the mind. And your mind is powerful beyond your wildest imaginings.

We're told that the most brilliant person on the earth uses but a fraction of his capacity. As yet, we don't even know how to unleash most of this great potential, but we know it's there. If you've read of the forgotten memories that people can call back and the unusual things they can do under medical hypnosis, you have a glimpse of what's locked inside us.

The power is obviously vast, and we can channel at least part of it by having proper attitudes. A positive, optimistic attitude about your potential will unlock a great deal of that power. This unlocking allows you to try harder, and though you won't achieve perfection, you will get much further than if your attitude holds you back.

Of course life is a challenge. That's what it was meant to be. But look at some of the dictionary meanings of the word *challenge:* an invitation to participate in an event; something that stimulates and excites; a dare.

If you foster attitudes in yourself that see life as that kind of challenge—a stimulating, daring invitation—you will enjoy the opportunities it brings you for growth and success.

Conclusion

Life is out there, just waiting. Whether you will charge into it and succeed or just wait listlessly for things to happen to you will make all the difference. The choice is yours.

Choices and consequences—freedom and responsibility— these are what success is all about. You're free to choose. You're free to become. Value your gift of choice, and make wise use of it. Then, be willing to take the consequences of your choices. Value your freedom and be willing to grow in the responsibility it demands, and you can't fail.

INDEX